THE UNEXPLODED BOER

Published by Zebra Press
an imprint of Random House Struik (Pty) Ltd
Reg. No. 1966/003153/07
80 McKenzie Street, Cape Town, 8001
PO Box 1144, Cape Town, 8000 South Africa

www.zebrapress.co.za

First published 2011

1 3 5 7 9 10 8 6 4 2

Publication © Zebra Press 2011
Text © Erich Rautenbach 2011

All rights reserved. No part of this publication may be reproduced, stored in a retrieval system or transmitted, in any form or by any means, electronic, mechanical, photocopying, recording or otherwise, without the prior written permission of the copyright owners.

The sources on page 141 constitute an extension of this copyright page.

PUBLISHER: Marlene Fryer
EDITOR: Robert Plummer
PROOFREADER: Beth Housdon
COVER DESIGNER: Michiel Botha
TEXT DESIGNER: Monique Oberholzer
TYPESETTER: Monique van den Berg
PRODUCTION MANAGER: Valerie Kömmer

Set in 10.5 pt on 15 pt Minion

Printed and bound by Interpak Books, Pietermaritzburg

ISBN 978 1 77022 165 9 (print)
ISBN 978 1 77022 207 6 (ePub)
ISBN 978 1 77022 208 3 (PDF)

Over 50 000 unique African images available to purchase
from our image bank at www.imagesofafrica.co.za

Dedicated to the memory of my mother, Shirley Graham, who gave me life and then saved it on countless occasions.

Similarity to any persons living or dead or presently engaged in the process of reincarnation is purely accitentional, though in some places names may have been changed to protect the guilty. There are some real people in here whose names I borrowed as a sort of tribute. Those names might be real. Well, maybe. Anyway, if real people do exist and their names have been changed, then they will know who they are. But this is really just a story, an allegory with ... umm ... archetypical overtones set in a country that no longer exists. Also, some of the places changed their names in the time that followed, because for a while the land had entered a fictional world of temporary names, and many names are being remembered again, some being forgotten, others living on in infamy like used toilet paper in a dry gutter.

But what's in a name anyway?

★★★★★★★ CONTENTS ★★★★★★★

	Preface xi
1	The End 1
2	Cuffed and Clueless 5
3	Windmills of My Mind 9
4	The Lucky City 19
5	The Slippery Slope 29
6	Hip Cats and Hobos 40
7	Die Kind van die Wind 47
8	The Psych Ward 55
9	Should I Stay or Should I Go? 68
10	Take the Money and Run 73
11	The Plan 81
12	Poison Runs 87
13	The Last Trip 92
14	John Vorster Square 97
15	Carl 109
16	A Guy Can Go Far in Fifty Seconds 114
17	Zip Nolan 127
18	The Pussy Posse Comes to Town 131
19	Insanity 140
20	The Fort 147
21	The Fort Hospital 152
22	Sterkfontein Sanatorium 161

23	On the Run	171
24	After I Escaped	177
25	Pretoria	180
26	While I Was Sleeping	185
27	Heroes	192
28	Homecoming	197
29	Royal Flush	205
30	When You Go Away	212
31	The Beginning	223
	Acknowledgements	231
	Translations	233
	Glossary	235

PREFACE

Time. Is this the time for a story? All I have, now, is a little old story from a long time ago, but old becomes new as the wheel turns round. I first wrote this story in the northern autumn of 1976 when I was in a hospital in a village somewhere in the Aquitaine region in France, home to the finest prune plums on the planet. It seemed like the first time I had stopped moving, stopped running, for years.

I was immobile, with a full leg cast, so the nurses brought me the yellow paper from between the X-ray photos and gave me pencils and I wrote the story by hand, with accompanying sketches. For two and a half months I wrote. Every detail, every person, was fresh in my mind. Time has weathered my memory and many of the gargoyles have long since dropped from the temples of my imagination, so much may have changed in the telling over the years since that version.

The thing is ... I was trapped in another demanding storyline and, after leaving the hospital on an 800-kilometre motorcycle ride with a kid named Frédéric, I ended up in a situation in Paris in early 1977 ... the time of the Ramones, Serge Gainsbourg, Patti Smith, Alain Stivell ... with this guy, Malik the Moroccan, who cleaned his nails with a stiletto knife and lived in an apartment in Saint Michel with two greasy sidekicks and three Doberman pinschers.

To this picture we add the words: I owed him money.

I had to leave Paris in a hurry, and very carefully, because Malik

THE UNEXPLODED BOER

wasn't the only dodgy customer in my life, and in the ensuing *disparu* I forgot about my manuscript, which is probably still somewhere in Paris. Here is some of what I remember…

THE END

'This,' muttered the small, dark-haired man, 'is a Parabellum with dum-dum bullets.'

A what?

The entire natural world seemed to anticipate his words before he spoke them. The clear, cold sunlight played through the trees, fracturing like in one of those Bergman movies that film buffs would watch at the old Labia Theatre on Orange Street in Cape Town, where the street curves near the Mount Nelson Hotel with its colonnades and tall palm trees.

He said it so softly. He didn't shout. Perhaps he had rehearsed that line for months in front of the mirror at his mother's house, angling his face this way and that, flipping up the collar of his jacket, adjusting the light and hoping to look cool to … whom – to me? *Is this some fantasy script, me just a bit player in his personality opus? What the fuck is the point of telling me the make or the specs of his gun?*

I lowered my gaze from his face and saw the object in his hand. It was pointed directly at my head through the open window of the Volkswagen. *Shit!* The morning sun glinted on the dull metal. My hung-over brain tried to catch up with his statement as I sat there in the passenger seat with the money and the dope in my lap.

I wouldn't even have pegged him for a cop, with the standard joller look about him, the slightly cool mullet, leather jacket and earring. Like a small-town guy trying hard to be hip in the big city.

The money was in a cloth bag with the Standard Bank logo. I flicked my eyes to the side and all my friends were gone, way down in the yard. They knew to move away when guns were in play …

When I'd woken up that morning things were weird, but when you are young and stupid you get used to the weirding of things. That morning I woke up in Endicott's garage, which was separate from the house, at the end of the driveway. Now, I admit that I had at times regained consciousness in funny places after I'd just got too tired and crawled away like some animal to lay down my weary head, but this was indeed one of the oddest. I woke up under a pile of wood, lumber, planks. While I was sleeping, somebody had covered me in wood, a big heavy pile of it. Not just a few pieces, but enough for a fence-building party. Who the hell would do that?

Early in the morning, I'd wriggled my way out of the woodpile and staggered out of the garage, babelas from the bottle of brandy I'd been drinking the evening before but feeling okay, young and strong. Life – let's do it again! I went out into the sunny chill of late autumn and across to the kitchen.

'Hey, where the heck were you last night?' Endicott asked in a slightly accusing tone.

'I was here, I got tired and fell asleep in the garage,' I countered. 'It's been a long trip. I'm sorry, man.'

'Bullshit. We looked for you in there, but nobody found you, and Donny took off,' he stated flatly.

'I was covered in wood,' I said. 'Who did that?'

'I have no idea what you're talking about. Maybe you should cut back on the drinking.'

'Maybe. I just want to get this finished and leave this place, Endicott,' I explained wishfully. 'I just want to get to my life. This is my last trip and then I'm going, getting the fuck out of here.'

THE END

'Ja well, they're gonna come back this morning, my brother and his friends. Want some coffee?'

'Naah, I just need some tea and a cigarette and I'll be okay.'

'This is a Magnum .357,' said a second cop as he leant through the driver's window and stuck a huge gun in my face. I turned and looked into two hard eyes, set close together in a big meaty head, staring down the barrel and ready to fire at the target – me. 'Now run!' At that moment universes disintegrated. Futures fell apart. Possible futures became never.

There are moments like this. Slices in time cut from the cake of destiny when you look up from your picnic, a gentle scattering of baguette crumbs on your lower lip and an empty glass of wine dangling askance in your hand as you observe, slightly surprised, as if it is just … a dream, the first wave of bombers, the nuclear flash, the volcanic eruption, and before you can reach out to touch it, to say goodbye, to linger for a moment over cherished secrets, your life, in a flash – gone.

Run? Did he really want me to run? Would he shoot me in the back, I wondered, or just the legs? We all knew it was a five-year minimum sentence for the first offence of 'Dealing in Dagga'. I put my hands in the air.

In the bright autumn sunlight I saw, through the windscreen of the burgundy Volkswagen, drums hanging from the leafless peach trees, strange fruit indeed, drums freshly airbrushed with beams of light refracting through a prism, the cover art of *Dark Side of the Moon*. Just ten metres from me, my friends waited for my world to end so that they could get back to their own good lives. They waited for the quicksand to close over my head. And on the tape deck in the Volkswagen, David Bowie sang, '*Five years, that's all we've got, We've got five years.*'

'You are under arrest,' the Big Man spat at me, as if daring me to argue.

3

'*We've got five years, that's all we've got*' … as long as I don't get raped or stabbed in the showers … as long as the judge is in a good mood. That's five years *minimum*, David my china, but the maximum depends on whether you cooperate with the authorities, and I was never very good with authority … or cooperation. (Doesn't play well with bullies.) More like ten years … and when you are twenty years old, ten years is as good as forever.

'I give up,' is all I could say. 'You win.' And I surrendered, *but I lied; I never gave up.*

The End. That is the end of this story, of this little chapter in my life, for sure. The beginning of my life was over and the end had just begun. Big fat end. Fridge falls out of the sky crushing hope into the concrete pavement. Ha ha ha ha. So funny. Twenty years old and the house just folded. This James Bond just got out-Jamesed. The big boys! The fucking end! *Finish an' klaa' my bra!*

CUFFED AND CLUELESS

They handcuffed me, yanking my arms behind my back, the metal grating my wrists, and shoved me into the back seat of an unmarked police car. Where were Endicott and the guys? The cops brought Endicott's brother and his friend and sat them on either side of me. They were the ones who'd set me up. They must have been. They'd brought these armed officers of the apartheid state to me.

These 'friends' of Endicott's brother had been introduced to me as *lang-gat jollers* from Boksburg who wanted to buy everything I had left. The more the better. I didn't suspect a thing. We were standing out of view from the street, next to the car by the garage, and I had shown them a sample so that they could see how fresh and tangy it was, all the time digging myself deeper into the hole. I was so proud of having the best stuff at unbeatable prices.

In Durban I had picked up a dozen classic white clay chillums to hand out to select customers and three corncob pipes especially for Donny. We were serious about smoking and in the cubbyhole we had three of the clay pipes and all of the corncobs pre-loaded and ready to smoke. Wherever we went we got people *lekker gerook*. I got in the car and offered them a pipe to try, but they declined, saying they could already see the good quality and didn't want to drive stoned. This was a new twist to me, but I put it down to Joburg, a city where people were often a little otherwise.

The guy with the earring counted out the money and put it in my hand. I deposited the loot in my moneybag and pulled out the stash from behind the front seat, breaking out the rolls of *gif*, feeling so happy and buoyant to finally be done with the heavy business of commerce. Then they went and ruined it all by pulling guns and getting so fucking serious. Suddenly they were the happy ones, and my life went to shit.

Two more cops turned up, a black one and a white one, who must have been covering the perimeter in case I made a run for it.

'So who's the cops and who's the robbers?' I wryly asked them, the police and my 'friends'.

Did Endicott know? Did he know that his brother was … what? An informer? An undercover cop in a police state? I thought he was my friend. Was Endicott an informer too, or complicit in some other way? Or would he be just as surprised to see his brother bringing the police to his house? I'd sold him a couple of fat rolls of Durban Poison, which were hidden outside the back door under the doghouse.

You can never tell in a police state. You do some little thing wrong and they threaten to lock you up and throw away the key unless you help them. Nothing much – just a few names, the odd phone call – and then you can go on living the life of the Happy White People, eating pizza and listening to Miles Davis, Bad Company or Cat Stevens. In the police state nobody looks. Nobody comments on the ripples on the pond.

'Hey, *takhaar*, where's the key to the Volkswagen?' the big one asked me. I had, in fact, slipped the key out of my back pocket and was busy hiding it behind the seat of the police car.

'I don't know, I don't have it,' I whispered, I croaked. In the distance I saw a tsunami of depression rise up and engulf the city of gold, Egoli. Darkness was everywhere that bright sunny morning. It was really starting to hit me, the enormity of what had happened, what was happening. The irreversibility of life.

Donny had the other key to the Volksie, but he'd slipped away while I was doing the deal, pretending to go and buy some wine around the corner, and disappeared. He'd seen something fishy in the whole play and he'd got out, which was a very good thing because he had nothing to do with my mission. I was just riding with him and giving him petrol money. He was on holiday from his regular job as a fireman, with a wife and baby back home.

Donny and I go back to the days of the Long Street musical tribes, back to when I was just a lightweight, a laaitie of fifteen, maybe 1969. My friend Phil, who gave me my first Bob Dylan record and played with me in my first rock 'n' roll band, was playing bass with some older guys called the Jimmy P. Freak Blues Band, with Donny on drums and The Twins on guitar. It was my first introduction to The Office on Long Street.

Betrayal was the last thing on my mind. I suppose I was quite naive, but I regarded my good friend Endicott's house as a trusted place and, by extension, his brother as 'one of us'. Maybe if I wasn't so obsessed with getting rid of the stuff and getting away to my imagined new life I would have picked up little signals. I was living in the future, my eyes firmly on my goal, instead of 'in the moment', and reality had arrived with all cylinders firing and a Be Here Now (like it or not) punch to the guts.

'Hey, Jew,' the big cop said impatiently to the smaller detective in his Afrikaner Joburg accent, 'get him out the fucking car and search him.'

'Out, out, out!' the other cop shouted at Endicott's brother's friend as he pulled him roughly from the vehicle, letting him fall to the gravel so I could get out. Only then did I notice, as the guy lay on the ground with his head twisted, that his face and neck were severely bruised like he had just been in a bad fight. I was only wearing a T-shirt, jeans and takkies and there wasn't much to search. The cop undid one of the handcuffs and made me turn my front pockets inside out and then he patted me down, feeling the very back pocket where the key had been a few minutes before.

'Take your shoes off and shake them out,' he commanded. I did so and waited for him to order me to drop my trousers but, thankfully, that was not their style. When they couldn't find the key anywhere on me they just let the air out of the tyres and left Donny's Volksie there in the driveway. As the police car was reversing out of the driveway, Endicott's girlfriend came running from the house with a big purple knitted jersey which they allowed her to give me, something I was going to be very grateful for during the long cold nights that followed.

★★★★★★★★★★★★ **3** ★★★★★★★★★★★★

WINDMILLS OF MY MIND

The day before the end, Donny turned the purple four-door Volkswagen into the driveway of the house in Parktown North, a residential area on the north side of Johannesburg. We had been staying on the other side, at a friend's flat down in the city, for almost a week, trying to get my business done. Before that we had driven all the way from Cape Town, 1600 kilometres up the coast to Durban and into the Zululand hills, and then inland another 600 kilometres to Joburg. I had done the trip often, and in many different styles and modes, from hitch-hiking in sandals to sitting in a jet plane with a Johnnie Walker lunch.

So there I was, back in the house where I had lived with Endicott, Granola Boy, the Joker, El Cid and QT. I had played drums in the band with Endicott and Granola Boy. The house was part of the Johannesburg rock music scene. People dropped by, partied together, had impromptu jam sessions and often hung out doing nothing in particular, just being cool, young and hip. That's where I met Julian, the guitar player from Freedom's Children (my favourite South African psychedelic metal band when I was about fifteen), and I got to jam regularly with hotshot guitarist Trevor Rabin, who would later write 'Owner of a Lonely Heart', which became a big hit for the prog-rock group Yes.

When I first got to Joburg, I was treated with respect by other musicians, compared to my home environs, where the top musicians were very much in isolated cliques. I almost couldn't believe it. People liked me for what I did. They liked the way I played, my no-nonsense businesslike beats. Of course, I didn't have a job and had no idea how to get one. I was way, way out in the cosmos, with all kinds of mental hang-ups and no confidence to boot – except when it came to drumming. People I admired liked me and wanted to jam with me, those musicians I'd watched on stage and who had inspired me, but I still never quite made it on the Joburg scene because I never had the Cash to Flash.

A few people took me aside and said I should get a regular job, but I couldn't, because the rumour was that the Evil Racist Government had just bought some very big Siemens computers from Nice Not-Nazi Germany and working a regular job would have put me into that computer system and alerted the authorities connected to the military. That is why I had gone to Johannesburg in the first place. Hiding from the military was my job.

Around the age of nineteen I'd had a relatively steady job in my home town of Cape Town, but the army got wind of me and sent my second set of call-up papers to my mother's house and I figured I had to leave. My job had been pretty cool, training as a blockman, learning to take apart whole pigs and beef hindquarters in a butcher's shop, but also all the smaller tasks like making hamburger patties, pumping sausages from the sausage machine, soaking hams in big barrels of brine, and hanging biltong and droëwors in the drying shed. This butcher also had a ship chandler's licence and a warehouse of beef and booze, which was where the real money was, so I worked a lot of the time at Cape Town harbour with the smells of the ocean mixed with oil and trains. We delivered supplies to ships from all over the world, mountains of beef and case upon case of wine and brandy for Dutch, Korean, Japanese and English freighters. Sometimes, when the weather was bad, the ships couldn't make port and we would have to do it by helicopter, taking out heavily stacked pallets dangling on a line, the wind howling and the seas reaching for the sky.

I had a girlfriend too.

Her parents were the ones who ran the business, and her lovely mother had taken me aside one day and told me that there was 'room in the company' for me. That was an offer, a doorway to a world that included me in the family with happily-ever-after thrown in for good luck if I wanted to step up to the plate. An ancient contract, a sacred compact, was being suggested: marriage, work, children. *Mate with my daughter and be one with my tribe.* Or maybe she was just offering me a job …

It is so funny in a film noir way. Inside I was feral and dark in ways that others could not comprehend. How did I make it through the sixties? I'd turned thirteen and entered puberty in 1967, the Summer of Love. Peace, Love and Grooviness. Make Love Not War was what my generation's role models told us to do. And if that wasn't enough they invented the miniskirt just to emphasise the point.

I was literally a child of the sixties. Love and miniskirts. Puberty, miniskirts, a windy city and double-decker buses. My legs still get weak at the thought of it. I had hair and bangles and bell-bottoms. But I still did not get it. Love and peace. I heard the words. (Did I mention the miniskirt?)

Trouble at work began when the spokesman of the brown people at the butcher's shop complained to the lady, the *marram*, the *missus*, about my behaviour and so she took me aside and spoke to me about it. The complaint was that I was using the toilet designated for the brown people, which was an outhouse right next to the toilet for the white people, exactly the same in all respects, and this made them uncomfortable because they thought I might be spying on them for the big white boss, her husband. I said I wouldn't do it again. This was the polite apartheid of middle-class Cape Town. These lovely folks had emigrated from England and created a good life for themselves. They didn't want to rock the boat. I was a native son and I just wanted to tear the fucking house down. Then the army tracked me down again.

Roberta Flack. 'The First Time Ever I Saw Your Face'.

But inside was something else. The darkness. I was a beautiful savage in the land of the teenage innocents. I tried my hardest to think positive and have good vibes. It was about Lessons in Love. *Lessons in love are free said she, then she took me by the hand, and showed me how to stand, saying lessons in love they are free.* I learnt nothing but I saw a glimmer. I was showered in a waterfall of love and I could not come clean.

Melanie. 'Brand New Key'.

My lovely girlfriend's belief is what tapped on my dark door. Most people could not see the darkness in me, because on the outside I was the complete opposite. I was young and handsome, so beautiful that girls pointed when I walked in the street. Boyfriends fumed with hatred. Prostitutes pretended to faint when I passed them. Older men still made moves on me, often from the safe confines of their cars as they cruised by, but I was no longer a twelve-year-old victim and I usually responded to their advances by kicking dents in their cars or smashing their windows with whatever I could find.

When I tried to explain the dark thoughts inside me, people refused to believe me. They told me I was talking nonsense, because I was beautiful and young, and they seemed to think that this made me immune to dark thoughts. 'You have so much!' they exhorted. I wished that my body was emaciated, dwarfed, crippled, hunchbacked, so that people could see the true me. No one believed me. Today you might say I suffered from anxiety or depression, but we did not possess those socially approved words back then.

The girl was good at what she did, and a mark was left on me, a seed of something, but it confused the hell out of me. Inside me it was simple. I felt bad. Very, very bad, and I wanted to feel good. Sometimes wine made me feel good, sometimes music or the open road. Girls made me feel good; the human contact, the simple touch of a human being, helped the bad feelings go away. I didn't know how it worked but it felt okay.

Songs for Beginners, Graham Nash. *I just want to hold you, I don't want to hold you down.*

Then the girl talked to me of Love and all my alarm bells flashed, exit signs sprouted everywhere and panic set in. Suddenly I was a lost puppy in downtown traffic, where the buses loomed larger and trucks belched smoke, people shouted, laughed and threw stones, and taxi drivers called out, honking their metal monsters, as thousands of razor-billed seagulls swooped down to attack me.

Love to me was death, and marriage was war. Love equalled unhappiness in the biggest dollops available. The girl stepped into the traffic of the downtown madness that was screaming in my brain and told me that it was okay. It was just a gift; it was the first gift, the oldest one, a seed, a simple gift from a friend, and there were no strings, and I felt so stupid, because I couldn't really understand.

She was a Beautiful Girl, trailing dreams and smiles, filled with the joy of life – a missionary, a believer in the all-conquering beauty of Love. Unselfish and generous. I couldn't take the gift. My hands were tied. Even if there'd been no war, no conscription, I still could not do it.

To me life was a sick joke and love was just a word, a filthy word that brought bad luck and twisted your soul with guilt and tears and pain. The concept of family was a hollow lie, marriage a curse spat with venom and hatred.

I was sick and infected. I had no hope and … I think I might have tarnished those dreams of hers, broken the last cherished vase of childhood perfection as she bestowed her gift upon me. Of all the beliefs in the world, a young girl's belief in love is perhaps one of the most delicate and beautiful things. If you have ever been lucky enough to be the recipient, or even just to see young girls in love passing in the street, the park, on the bus, you must know what I mean.

I trampled carelessly in holy places.

In the end, the arrival of my army papers tipped the scales of confusion and one day I just disappeared and went to Johannesburg. I didn't say goodbye. I had no idea how to. I went away wordlessly, but I took with me the memory, and in dark places I would take it out and torment myself with raw emotions and ponder the significance of the resulting tears. It took a while – well, actually a very long time – for me to realise that I had some control over my own thoughts and didn't have to hate myself forever. But it was a start, a chink in my dark curtain that fed doubt and held me back from my daily suicidal thoughts, from my final plan of self-termination.

Even in my darkness I dreamed of going to university, but I had left high school, dropped out, just before my final exams, overwhelmed by some kind of futility, the whole trip, the sixties, peace, love and oh-my-god, my fucked-up family, racist government, police state, oppression. Overshadowing all was the army. All the way through high school, certain teachers had rubbed their hands in glee, telling me that the army was going to break me and that I was just the type that they would crush into bone dust. I have to credit my foul-mouthed gym teacher Mr Snowman for convincing me that those guys would, in all likelihood, kill me.

So, apart from my general personal crisis, the government wanted me to report for duty and pick up the gun to fight for apartheid, to join the unquestioning propagandised drones and be bonded to 'my people' through guilt and blood. As soon as I got a job, The Government would know where I was and would send the military police, who would take me to stand trial for evading military service and, after I had done my prison time, I would be put in the army where they would do all they could to break me down. They had permission and I was breakable, more fragile than I let on. I would have been good entertainment for those low-grade military motherfuckers.

Obeying my call-up seemed a stupid thing to do. I mean, if I was going to fight for something, why not fight against the bad guys? But that's ... us. Civil war. Dirty business.

If you had asked me at the time, I would have told you that I wanted to fight for the other side. I had no idea what the other side was, but from the propaganda that our government filtered through my young mind, it seemed that the other side was *Communism*, masterminded by the evil chief of World Communism called Russia, the Soviet Union, the USSR. The Russians gave weapons to 'freedom fighters', so they were on the same side as me. But still, what was my side? The nice guys? Liberals? Leftists? Socialists? Democrats? Blacks? Whites? Browns? Young? Old?

I had never heard of the African National Congress. I grew up in the big quiet time. The name Nelson Mandela was never mentioned at my school, in my home or among my friends, and I didn't know that he was sitting in a cell on Robben Island just out there in the bay. I had no idea that Stephen Biko was criss-crossing the country, fomenting ideas of Black Consciousness among the youth. If you asked me at the time I said stuff like: 'If I was a black cat' – we said *cat* then, not *dude* – 'I would secretly kill whites all the time,' or 'I am going to go to Russia and I'll come back with a liberating army.' But who would I liberate? I felt oppressed because I lived in a police state that wanted to force me gang-style to put on its colours and kill for it. I didn't relate to 'my people'.

I was raised outside of my tribe, the Afrikaners. My surname was Afrikaans, but my mother was 'English'. English was my mother tongue. I had never heard of Commandant Rautenbach of the Bethlehem Commando who rode with General Christiaan de Wet during the Anglo-Boer War and later was one of the '*bittereinders*', guerrillas who vowed to fight till the bitter end against the vicious British tyrants. Men who ate their horses, their saddles and their leather clothes to stay alive as 100 000 English bastards hunted for the last 700 'freedom fighters' of the Boer nation.

I was a young guy with foolish ideals and immature political understanding. Though I said I wanted to fight for the other side, I really knew nothing about it. The government told us through the chicken-shit fake media that the black revolutionaries were just misguided pawns tricked by the filthy communists. I have fallen for a lot of lies in my life but I didn't buy that crock. I was still confused, though, because the only version of information available was controlled totally and I knew it. I had to invent the truth. That was the only place to find it.

These were the years before the 1976 Soweto uprising and the subsequent massacre that set the country aflame. But in this time, when I was young, people told me I was crazy (true), I was a coward (possibly) or I just didn't like the idea of army discipline (definitely) – but there was *no way that any black person could or would ever be able to run any damn country. They're just too stupid!* That was the usual rap.

This was my time, the time of Grand Apartheid, the perfection of the system, after Nelson Mandela had been put in prison and all public dissent broken and silenced, when I was about seven years old, a period that ended on 16 June 1976 when the pus bubbled over in an eruption after the police started shooting the children in the name of the Afrikaans language.

After that day it was out in the open and nobody could avoid the ugly truth till democracy, already gang-raped by the Western world, staggered into the arena eighteen years later.

But in those years there was no dissent. None was allowed. There were no strikes. No unions. No public gatherings of opposition. And there was definitely no talking in this class. We were the Happy White People. Behind this façade a great machine of repression toiled in all possible ways at all hours on everything it could think of. I grew up in those years.

It took me a long time to realise that I had been let down – not only by my 'own' people, because who really were my own people? I was a visible minority being forced to kill people by a colonial cult of thugs. Where were my leaders? Where were the leaders of the country? Besides the ones who were in prison, it seemed that many of them were in London, smoking cigars and going to banquets to raise money while their children went to the finest schools in the world.

They never reached out to us – the teenagers destined to kill the black youth. They never sent any pamphlets or missionaries. There were no secret messages in the South African rock and pop songs. All we had for reference were young American artists saying a definitive 'no' to war in Vietnam and singing about brotherhood, civil rights and peace.

These were the days before the End Conscription Campaign. Never once while I was growing up or travelling around the country, not once was there a pamphlet or a piece of paper telling me about the truth. Not one scrap of evidence that they wanted me not to be a soldier of apartheid.

No, I was condemned to be trapped in the racist reality, the white toilet. I mean, I can understand not wanting 'whitey' in their organisations, because they had been hampered and tricked and betrayed so often by going along with white liberal half measures, but we were just kids. I think the leadership of my time was non-existent within the borders of South Africa. People were ruled by fear. The adults of all colours were quaking in their boots, pissing in their socks.

And, believe me – you would too if the bad guys came to your town.

I knew no one who had similar thoughts to me. It was my own private war. I was young and limited by my bouts of melancholy and didn't have anything in the way of mentors, because of my inability to communicate effectively or ask for help, or proper role models; I just had distant and imaginary figures from the seductive media. Characters like Muhammad Ali, who said no to military service in Vietnam and was sent to prison, sacrificing his reputation and career for a principle, or Captain Devil, tawdry hero of the fabulous propaganda *poesboekies* who killed 'terrorists' by the dozen for his country but was driven half-mad and alcoholic in the process. I had to make up my own mind about things. I had to use my eyes to send information to my brain and then come up with an answer. My answer was that I had no right to be there because I was 'white'. Because I had light hair and blue eyes it seemed obvious to me that I came from some other place and should go back there, and then there would be one less gun and one less pair of boots.

It was simplistic racist thinking. It had never even occurred to me that my very blood from my father's family could be anything but 'pure white', and I might be somebody who actually had a right to be some place on this earth.

THE LUCKY CITY

Cape Town is my home town. That's the way it was and always will be. But I wasn't born there; my papers come from the far north. My parents got married in Cape Town (Rondebosch to be exact), but they were always on the move in the fifties, following the jobs, trying to make ends meet, riding the deserts and crossing the colonies in pre-war British cars with big mudguards and chrome headlights like the 1936 Riley or the 1934 Alvis.

I was born where the desert meets the ocean in Swakopmund, Namibia, then called South West Africa. I almost died from diarrhoea and dehydration, something to do with the groundwater, and the doctors gave my mother medicine to save my life, but, being an avid Christian Scientist at the time, she threw away the *muti* and instead fed me bottles of rooibos tea and faith and luckily I made a good recovery.

My father had spent some time in Windhoek before, on his first journey to Namibia around 1951. Being very arty he soon came into contact with a group of painters from Germany, all Jewish, who had fled to Africa to escape the Holocaust. Even with the death camps and the Nazis still such a fresh memory, this small cadre of artists identified very strongly with German culture. They loved the Germany that had been home to their families for generations, and they missed it terribly. When they met my father and heard his surname, they told him that he had a great German name and should be proud of his heritage.

The name Rautenbach had been a Boer name 'for centuries'. My father only had the vaguest knowledge that way back in 1700-and-something a German, who scarpered from Europe, got off the Dutch *Compagnie* boat and married a once-divorced daughter of the good Portuguese man Ferreira, then had eight kids. The sons went forth and started a new tribe with fine shapely Dutch girls, cultured French girls and almond-eyed golden children of the earth, with mysterious spicy slave girls, proud dark daughters of mighty chiefs and peaches-and-cream beauties from England. The daughters blended into other tribes and two hundred years later the ancestral German culture was pretty much dissolved. Long gone. Only the name remained.

But, being the consummate artist that my father was, he entered his bloody German Phase and insisted on giving all his children names that would 'harmonise' to retain a Germanic flavour. So his three sons became Erich, Manfred and Helmuth, branded forever as krauts, square-heads and other such ridiculous terms that were tossed about in those times. All the war comics we read had the Germans losing. All the movies we saw had the Germans losing. An entire new genre of villain was created both in fiction and in reality. The Nazi and the war criminal.

And so this is a good time to give your kids German names?

We lived in a former British colony and we spoke English. An English name would have been good. Or how about a nice Boer name? A little something from Africa? But no, we'll just go German.

Fucking Adolf Hitler! I blame him for that. I blame him for chasing those nostalgic Jewish painters into the desert to fill my dad's head with their Teutonic titillation which induced in him a romantic nineteenth-century Prussian officer daydream. Often he would call me Baron Erich von Rautenbach and click his heels.

But hey, what's in a name? I would clock my heels in response and nod my head in my usual curt baronial fashion.

I don't know how long we stayed in Namibia, but my earliest conscious memories are all the way south, in the Cape, when we were living in Clovelly on the mountainside just outside Fish Hoek. We had dogs with big ticks. One day while playing with my brother on the high stoep I took a fall which resulted in a rock sticking into my forehead. Once again, doctors and medicine were ignored in favour of prayer and faith and I still have a scar at my hairline that makes me look like I've had a minor frontal lobotomy.

Apparently those were lean years for architectural drafting and the jobs were short-lived, over once the projects were completed. We moved around fast: to Jonkershoek outside Stellenbosch, north again to Windhoek in Namibia, and back to Cape Town.

This time we landed in the village of Fish Hoek, where we moved around a few times, ending up in a house called Avoca. The summers were endless; the beach and the glittering ocean became my daily hangout. When I was six or seven my older brother and I would walk the hot pavements to the beach, rolling our old patched-up inner tubes, and we'd ride the foamy end of the waves as they lapped the shore. Right down on the beach right next to the sand dunes, between the railway tracks and the ocean, were the old whitewashed cottages of the fishing families. Occasionally they would bring in a catch of yellowfin tuna, and we would go into the water and pull together, knee-deep in the surf, until the big net was hauled onto the beach bristling with big fat fish, crabs and jellyfish. People came from their cars to buy the fish right there on the beach. Fresh from the ocean.

In Fish Hoek I had my most exceptional days of schooling. For the first two years (called Sub A and Sub B back then), in a tiny schoolroom blocks away from the big primary school, I won all the little prizes for *most outstanding work* and *most advanced work*. Top of the class. My glory days. It all went downhill after that, once I moved to the big school for Standard 1 (which is now called Grade 3) and met Mrs Forsyth. She had it in for me. It didn't matter that I could write and read better than anyone else in the class; she couldn't take it that

I hadn't learnt to sing the alphabet 'a-b-c-d-e-f-g' in a sing-song fashion. I read all my goddamn books from cover to cover on the first day of school. That wasn't good enough and she would mock me in front of the other kids.

At the end of that school year we skedaddled once more, to Stellenbosch again, where we stayed in some kind of 'rooms' in a house and I spent the first six months of 1963 at Paul Roos Gymnasium, a venerable establishment of Afrikaans education, with rugby fields as far as the eye could see. We didn't need to cross the line into Afrikanerhood to get schooled, as there was a special class for English-speaking kids, but the school did have stronger discipline than I was used to and the teachers had a fondness for hitting children with various bits of wood. Three words wrong in a spelling test and you received a whacking. This was shocking to me. Until then I had never been hit with wood by an adult, but luckily I had an affinity for words and a knack for spelling. Almost all the other kids in my class had English or European names. I was the only Afrikaans-challenged student with a Boer name, and some of the teachers automatically spoke Afrikaans to me.

We ran barefoot whenever and wherever we could, but not at school, because at school you always wore shoes. But at this school we saw kids walking in from outlying farms without any shoes on. This was scandalous to me – I had never imagined school without shoes and socks. They were wild Boers, some of the kids in my class said. Some others thought that they were just too poor and, even though they could get charity shoes, their feet had become so flat and wide from never wearing shoes that now they couldn't. Whatever the story, they were exotic. They were barefoot and couldn't speak English.

I loved the town, with its old buildings and monuments, and the smell of ripe fruit everywhere in summer, the parklands on the outskirts with scorpions and cobras hiding under rocks, the ice-cold Eerste River running silver under the trees on the hot summer days.

If we had remained in that university town, the home of Afrikaner intellectualism, and I had stayed on at that school, I could have made the jump into Afrikaans schooling. They would have liked me to do it. It was so close. We were so close. But then my family upped and moved again halfway through the school year. I was young and didn't see how difficult life was becoming for my parents, trying to get ahead, hopping from one place to another and remaining a family.

There were four kids now, and when I was nine years old we moved to Cape Town, ending up in a house on Moray Place in Oranjezicht. It wasn't too bad for about three years, even though we didn't have much money. I went to Tamboerskloof Primary School and on the weekends we walked up the mountain, or over Kloof Nek and down through The Glen to Camps Bay Beach, or we took the train to Muizenberg and Sandvlei where I would fish for harders and steenbras. Things were normal. I was a boy and the things my father did were magnificent and mysterious. I would sometimes go to the offices he worked in as some sort of draftsman, with the blueprints of buildings and the fancy pencils and pens, high chairs and drafting tables. Every Sunday I was brushed and scrubbed and went to the Sunday school, where I learnt about Israel and God and Jesus.

I met all the kids on my small block: Nicki and Julian the Polish boys on the corner of Upper Orange Street, Rudie and Heidi the German kids in the small green flats, John the English boy with the house near the stairs, and Johnno the Scot and his family in the third house connected to ours. And the kids from District Six.

Growing up in the heart of Cape Town, there in the Lucky City, it was impossible to stay immune to the ancient hobby of mixing races, no matter how hard they urged us not to, no matter how many laws they passed. Perhaps adults found it easier to live apart, but not children. It just wasn't … natural.

My relationship with the children of District Six, a brown and black peoples' neighbourhood just down the street, the very first and oldest urban neighbourhood in the country, perhaps the subcontinent, a truly historical area, started then, when I was just a boy. Until then nobody had told me anything about race. It hadn't occurred to me yet.

I had no idea that brown boys were 'different' from white boys.

I was maybe ten years old when I first met them on Mill Street, that gang of little boys of varying ages, one hot afternoon during the summer when the schools were closed for the six-week Christmas holidays and time stood still, mirages shining on the hot tar roads. There were always eight or ten of them, a bunch, and they would wander up from the District looking for me.

They usually found me down on the corner of Mill Street and Hiddingh Avenue, long before they built the Gardens Centre, sitting on the hot granite kerbstones, my feet in the gutter, sipping on an Iron Brew or a Cocopina by the old butcher's shop, or I'd be across from Varney's Grocery, leaning on the wall by the chemist at the bottom of Breda Street, or maybe across the road looking in the window at Katz's Bakery.

There was one summer in particular, but for the life of me I can't remember what the year was – possibly 1964 or '65. Before then I'd had an older brother, but the moment he went to high school he dropped me like a hot stone and the adventurous partnership that had existed between us since I was born was dissolved for all time.

It was in these wandering days, when I was alone for the first time in my life, that I met that group of kids. Perhaps, at first, people might have commented on the blond boy running with the brown boys, but District Six was home to every colour and some were quite like me, and, anyway, by the time we had scrambled through the pine tree sap and the gravel in the park, eating sticky sweets and running up and down all kinds of streets doing what boys do, picking things up and throwing them around, jumping, climbing, falling, rolling down grass hills, having fights with clods of grass, we were all the same colour. Whatever floated in the city or lay on the ground, we touched it and it stuck to us as surely as if it were pollen and we were bees.

We were the kings of the city, barefoot, dirty and free, and our empire stretched from Tamboerskloof to Vredehoek, from the Pipe Track to the Foreshore. I remember those times we spent at the docks. While the vehicles were being checked at customs we would slip by and take over the area.

We ran from the big docks to the little docks and watched when the fishing trawlers came in. We knew the names of the tugboats. We ran through huge warehouses and under monstrous cranes as they swung giant loaded arms. We rode on the backs of trains as they shunted and we traded gossip with sailors from other countries.

We had a secret place where we would hang out, fishing and eating chips from the greasy spoon down there at the Duncan Dock. Here and there, in the bustling grown-up business of the international port, where goods flowed to the world and big people moved big things, here and there were doorways, portals into a secret world. You just had to know where to look.

One doorway that we used took us under the harbour, under the wharves, and into a shadowy network of beams and pilings, huge timbers, the dark water shifting below. We would climb into this underworld and across those timbers. The sun would poke through in places, making startling light shows, exposing shoals of little silver fish banking left and right, and the water was that particular colour of warm green. There were seals or porpoises swimming there, away from the tugboats and oil slicks and the ever-competitive seagulls. It was like a private aquarium and we would lie on the beams dangling three-cornered hooks, trying to catch the sleek silver harders as they swarmed up to the breadcrumbs we dropped on the water.

The last time we ran together it was early one summer night, the tar of the pavement still warm and soft underfoot as we made our way down Orange Street, across from De Waal Park, by the old Deanery where the Anglican Dean of Cape Town lived with his many beautiful daughters. There was a dead area with a chain-link fence next to their house that led into a big unused chunk of real estate known in the annals of local kid lore as the Millys, and I liked to imagine that this was where the old mill had been, the one that ate all the old-growth trees before they planted the pines and left us with Mill Street.

The Millys was legend for all the bad things that could be done there. Cigarettes, booze, girls, violence. Our house, round the corner on Moray Place, backed onto the Millys too, and I had camped out there myself for three weeks when I was ten, playing truant, pretending to go to school but instead sneaking off to my camp, where I spent the day trying to catch field mice, using bits of my sandwich for bait. But on this night somebody else was intent on climbing through the hole in the fence to do bad things.

We saw this guy, already in the shadows, near the Crèche, the day-care for children, a well-dressed white guy with his arm around a woman, pulling her – no, pushing her – a very pretty, big-bellied, pregnant, brown-skinned young woman, her arm pinned. She was struggling, her eyes wide with fear and panic.

'Hey, mister!' one kid shouted.

The man jerked his head towards us. 'Fuck off, you kids,' he hissed. He put his hand in his pocket and threw a pack of cigarettes at us. Nobody picked them up.

'What you doing?' screamed another kid. We moved in closer, surrounding him with his hostage up against the Crèche wall.

'Hey, mister, what you doing? Hey mister, HEY MISTER!!??' We jumped up and down and all started shouting at the tops of our voices.

'Rape! Rape! Rape!'

'Police, police, police!'

'Raaaaaaaape!'

Lights started coming on, and it was obvious that the people in the houses would soon be out on the street to investigate the disturbance. The man gave an angry snarl as he removed his arm from the young woman's throat and pushed her at the wall. Then he bolted, diving through the circle of kids, running across Orange Street and making a left down Camp Street, his long legs carrying him fast. He knew the area well, and he crossed the street and slipped away from the lights, under the tall pine trees, and ran through the children's play park, past the swings and the roundabout, to the water reservoirs. He disappeared into the dark shadows under the stubby little palm trees as we followed, shouting, running, fanning out and hunting the fugitive.

It seemed he had made a left down Union Street and vanished. We trotted down the street and came upon the Oranje Hotel, a funny little hotel tucked away, with front and back entrances on two streets. We went around the back way onto Weltevreden Street and sneaked up to the window, peering in, and there was our guy, sitting at a table in the lounge and ordering a beer.

After a quick battle council, half the guys went around to the other side again and then we all burst into the bar, a dozen barefoot urchins, Crime Fighters of the Lucky City, and surrounded the Bad Man, humiliating him, fingering him, with the red-faced grown-ups freaking out.

'No children! No children!' shouted the hotel receptionist.

'You can't come in here,' hissed the waiter. 'Stop! Stop! This is for Whites Only.'

'Little *donders*, the police will *moer* you. Out! *Voertsek!*'

Then the manager stormed in. 'What are you doing? Everybody just shut up!'

Eventually the police were found cruising in the area, having already been called by the folks who had found the distraught young lady, and they took the embarrassed would-be rapist away. I made a statement to the blue-clad custodians of Law and Order and a few months later I received a summons and went to court and the assailant was given a nine-month suspended sentence.

I don't remember seeing that group of boys again. That all happened just before the government first started the ethnic cleansing in District Six.

Perhaps they were forcibly removed by uniformed Afrikaners out to Bonteheuwel or Manenberg, away from the old buildings, the history, the homes, or out to some place on the sand dunes with the tin shacks and the *vygie* plants, with the mountain and their memories as Creole Kings of the Lucky City, crime fighters and fishermen, way over there in the distance … almost obscured by the low-lying industrial clouds from the Mandrax pipes.

Ethnic cleansing. It was a crime we could not fight. We were still too small and the big people all seemed to be broken.

THE SLIPPERY SLOPE

At the age of eleven I used to climb up and sit in the loquat tree in the backyard of the house on Moray Place and dream that I did not belong in my family, that I was really of royal blood, from another place far away and that, 'one day soon', someone would come to rectify the situation, to set it all straight, and then I would go home.

Perhaps dislocation and not belonging has always been my fixed state or possibly it is the result of not being 'branded' into some society – circumcised, baptised, ritualised, confirmed, bar mitzvah'd, tattooed or otherwise inducted. Perhaps being the 'outsider' is just a twisted yearning to belong, a failed 'member' reconfiguring the thwarted hard-wired need to belong to a more complex social group. I had no sense, then, of 'being African', and I had no self-awareness of how physically bonded I was to the landscape and the sounds of language and the smells of the people, the earth, the trees, rocks and … everything. And I had only just begun.

Life was about to slide down the slippery slope.

My father left us, moving out just before I started high school, and my newly self-conscious mind suddenly became aware that we were in a bad way. We had been broke before but now we were broken and penniless as my mother made adjustments to her life. We were 'poor whites' living in the rented house on Moray Place with battle-scarred rats the size of dogs running in the walls and dying from the poison and stinking up the place for weeks. Suddenly I hated my life.

On top of that was The Lie. My mother told me to 'tell them nothing' about our family break-up, so when the school secretary asked me if my father was still at home I lied and said he was. They knew I was lying but I did it anyway. Every time they asked.

I remember being twelve years old, deserted by my father, while my mother screamed at me that it was 'all your fault, all your fault' that he had left. Again and again she drummed it into me. It sounds like a terrible thing for a mother to say to a child. It is, but it is understandable, even forgivable.

Everybody cracks up, loses it sooner or later, and with luck there are friends, family, tribal elders, social safety nets, to help put the pieces back together again. Sometimes you run out of luck. My poor mother was left to face the future on her own with four kids to feed, a job to find after fifteen years at home, and no people to help her. We were all swathed in a morose blanket of sadness, which happens to produce the scent that draws in the predators, lurking, waiting for one to drop behind. They pounce on the weakest and feed.

When the filthy creeping man came with hands to touch me, to burn away my purity and my innocence, I had no one to defend me, no one to call to for help. No person to take a knife and rip it into his guts left and right and up and down. All I had was guilt and hatred. Then the monster threw some gift to me, payment for the murder of my youth, trying to make me a whore, make it all my fault.

What do you do with an experience like that? You're hived off from the herd. You are given cultural confusion, shock, denial, and other things compressed together and the brain takes over and puts it all away. I somehow managed to hide the experiences from myself, farmed the evil into my psyche, polluted the green fields of my subconscious and lived off the resultant fruits, the bitter-tasting cynicism, the self-hatred and the anti-social behaviour.

I found a refuge in music. When I was just eleven or twelve, my mother had bought me a ticket to see the Beatles film *A Hard Day's*

Night, but even before that I had heard songs on the old valve radio in our house, drifting in from the background, impinging on the bubble of my childhood, calling me from that dreamland to the cold reality of the big world.

'Hang Down Your Head Tom Dooley'. The Seekers doing 'The Carnival Is Over'. Four Jacks and a Jill with 'Master Jack'. Chubby Checker belting out 'Let's Twist Again'.

These songs, they all floated around like a distant swarm, buzzing on the periphery, trying to enter my thoughts. I saw them, I heard them, in the background of the country of my dreams, like the Cold War and John F. Kennedy and the Suez Crisis, but I was still present in the big sleep, the happy dreamtime of childhood.

When that childhood was invaded by darkness and unhappiness, my life began to disintegrate. Then one day I heard a riff, a clarion call, a call to arms. I heard the pounding of the drums. I heard my national anthem coming out of the radio, 'Paint it Black' by the Rolling Stones, and it reached in to my childhood; it reached in and pulled me from the dreamland and I was found.

Music gave me life. Music reflected my thoughts and emotions. Music became my family, my church, my confidante, my secret friend, my mother-father, my mentor, my guide and my refuge.

My mother saw this, and she bought me a portable battery-operated record player along with *Wild Thing* by The Troggs and the four-song *Paint it Black* e/p by the Rolling Stones. I got some drum sticks and I banged on cardboard boxes and pots and my mother saw this so she went to the shop downtown that had financed her washing machine, the Hoovermatic with a spin dry, so we didn't have to do our laundry by walking on it in the bath any more, and she arranged to get a loan from these people, the home appliance shop next to the old Alhambra Theatre where I saw French pop star Johnny Halliday perform the Deep Purple song 'Hush' and fall off the stage and break his toe.

She took that loan and bought me an ancient British Carlton

drum kit with a set of bongos attached to the bass drum. That's what my mother did for me, the extraordinary lengths she went to. I had something to focus on. I believed implicitly in the dream, the power, the communal spirit of rock 'n' roll.

I practised those drums like crazy and from the age of fifteen I started playing in bands with guys from school. By the time I was sixteen I was in a band with some older cats who Poison Pete had introduced me to, and we played covers of hard-rock songs by bands like Rory Gallagher's Taste, Black Sabbath and Jethro Tull at dances and hotels around the city and in the suburbs. We even got to play at the big outdoor festival and battle of the bands at Hartleyvale Stadium in the summer of 1970 and at a rock festival in Goodwood where we were the first band, going on at midnight to the crowd of about five thousand early-bird hippies all relaxed on the hot night. As we kicked into the second song, we saw dozens of police rush in and drag away all the stoners they caught smoking. We played right through and, while we performed Black Sabbath's 'Iron Man', we watched as they whacked people on the head.

In early 1971 I left the group, because they needed a more experienced drummer and because I was already starting to work with my friend Johnno on original songs for the band Bottleneck. I didn't want to just do cover tunes. I wanted to be part of a band that said something. My old band had a hard time finding the right drummer and eventually they agreed to try my old school pal the Mighty Thwaites, who blew them away with his technique and groove. They changed their name to Wigwam and became a very popular powerhouse band with his amazing drumming.

Pop culture was the new religion. The era of the matinee idol was long gone. At the forefront of all things cool was the pop star, the rock artist. They were the new gods, and to be in a band, to be part of it all, was like joining an international religion, becoming part of the holy order.

Along with pop culture came drug culture, and suddenly everyone was smoking zol. Skyfing. They skyfed at the beach, in the park, down the alley, outside parties and in speeding cars. The smell was everywhere. When I was first playing drums, fifteen years old, I hung out at The Office on Long Street with the older cats who smoked weed, took black beauty speeders, played the boogie guitar all night long and then drove up the mountain to catch the sun rising.

As a teenager I spent a lot of time down near Caledon Square police station hanging in Squeaky's shebeen off Buitenkant Street, home of tantalising unlabelled white wines and the best zol in the city, and yes, sometimes in the District as I grew older, drinking tea as the sun came up with my friend who ran a crash pad for street prostitutes in an old warehouse, and up in the Bo-Kaap and a hundred other places where the Off-Grid People met, listening and watching, and so my identity was riddled with the backstreet talk of shebeen cats and alley brats.

Right from the beginning though, District Six was a no-go zone. It was a ghetto, off limits, whites not allowed in by law, but it was right there in the centre, surrounded on all sides by the beautiful Lucky City – this place where no money was spent, no beautification was done, where everything was old and stained, chipped and peeling, and teeming with life. I went a few times with friends to their houses in the District, had dinner with parents and so on, but there was this tension. Maybe it was different in the old days, but to bring a white friend home was trouble. Nobody was comfortable. 'It was just asking for it.' A lot of the guys hanging on the street would aggressively tune you shit like, '*Wie's jy? Ken jy vir die ding? Wut you wunt waaitie?*'

There was no going into the District at night, especially without a car. The police cruised up and down the streets looking for trouble, and young white guys were the favourite target. There was no escape when you were walking. The government gave them licence to be bullies in my village. You didn't have to do anything wrong. They were the hunters and they hunted for long hairs, and my blond hair shone bright in the night.

The truth is I was looking for trouble. I needed to buy weed and it just happened that it was the brown guys and black guys who controlled the supply. That's how I found my way to Squeaky's, which was set in a sort of no-man's-land of run-down village dwellings, all destined for destruction, in the heart of the old city on the edge of everything, where all colours blended.

At first it was just like any other merchant – in the door, ask for stuff, pay up and leave – but after a while they got to know me and when I came to pick up a parcel (*twee rand vyftig vir die arm*) for friends at school, Squeaky would pull out a big handful of *gunston* and in his falsetto voice would add, '*Hie's 'n paar koppe vir jou, Blondie.*'

After a while I got invited down the passageway and into the backyard to smoke pipe and *blow tjonna* down the wall. In the back there I saw how many bottles of wine he sold, unlabelled bottles of yellow see-through. I was a teenager then and didn't drink alcohol, but sometimes I would go into the back room and smoke a few with the hard-core losers, the homeless broken people who Squeaky allowed to hang there. I spent a lot of time there around age sixteen and seventeen in the afternoons after school. There were young and old people, alcoholics, cripples, amputees, thieves, prostitutes, drug dealers and even a few guys with jobs. There was talk. Always talk and laughter. They. We. All of us were on the wrong side of the law in some way or other, and just by existing, by being together, we were a conspiracy in action.

Quite a few guys were gang members – street gangs and jail gangs. They had a 26 or a 28 tattooed on a Bible on the inside of their forearms, from the infamous and legendary Number Gangs that operated within the prison system, but they never talked about it, though in the course of general conversation legends were passed around like an expensive bottle of brandy. Many of the stories revolved around people who talked to the police, the hated 'boere', the *befokte mapuza*, and people who didn't talk to the police when they were arrested.

Philosophies like these may exist in other cultures, perhaps among

Sicilian gangsters or First Nations smugglers operating between Canada and the United States. This was criminal survival philosophy in a country where educated and otherwise decent 'white' people, nice people who had been to university and collected art, read poetry, played sports and attended church and synagogue regularly, made laws stating that all those people were inferior and so should be deprived of the good life. They did not get the education, could not vote, had to live in certain areas and endure all sorts of perverted legal fuckery on the daily road to humiliation. This was Law as handed down over three hundred years by foreigners, invaders, settlers, colonials, capitalists and tourists of all natures.

This unwritten criminal code, the conscious 'us against them' mentality in these stories, seemed to me to be a constant form of civil rebellion, the only visible sign of life in this sickly country. The police were the enemy as eternal soldiers of the Overlord, and co-operation with them was the surrender of all that was holy.

It was war.

The unlucky people who 'talked' in these stories, after being beaten by police and blackmailed with the safety of their family, always ended up losing their heads, decapitated in a terrible act of off-road justice, and the people who didn't talk and served their slow prison time, who bore the hard weight of life on their shoulders, had their families looked after by the 'brothers'. Over time, the impeccable logic, the solid tribal dependency of that mythical philosophy became mine, just as surely as if I had gone to a Roman Catholic church four times a week and listened to a priest for years on end.

I loved the beauty, the logic, the Super-Clean Maths. It was a law that took shape in my head, and I carried it with me like a religion. I was from the Cape and down there 'we don't betray our brothers'.

I studied the same branch of Mathematics as they did and so I took their theorem with me wherever I went. *You don't leave your people. You don't desert them.*

In a world gone mad, you could build a home on that thought.

There weren't 'hard drugs' in evidence on the streets of Cape Town in those days. There were elite cliques that had access to medical morphine and little stashes of heroin and cocaine brought in from Europe. A large number of the girls at school in the late sixties and early seventies took prescription 'slimming pills', which were made from some kind of speed that kept them buzzing through the day with no appetite. The white adults, the parents, were heavily into Valium, the designer drug of the time that took the hard edge off living. LSD was available if you knew the right people, and later I would do a fair bit of that, but at first it was only zol.

We didn't have fancy glass pipes like the addicts have now, for chasing their dragons or sucking their speed or puffing a big dirty Mandrax cloud. Us, we smoked our zol, our *gunston*, in the bottleneck pipe, broken nicely in paper to make no mess and then the sharp edges ground dull. It was a communal affair. The bottleneck pipe is not for one man. Once you've got the bottleneck ready, you take the foil from a pack of smokes, fold it longways and then curl it up like a spring to make the 'diamond' in the bottom of the pipe. On top of that you set the 'backstop', a thin layer of tobacco to act as a filter and to let you know when the pipe is at its end. You mix up the *gunston* with the *sout* (some tobacco) to 'make it burn better', and fill up the pipe. *Rokers* who didn't smoke tobacco still carried cigarettes just to mix with the weed, often one of those small green and white packs of Cavalla Kings. Lastly, if you were civilised, you added a final filter, the *sofie*, a piece of cloth over the mouthpiece of the pipe. Many people could smoke on one pipe and a lot of smoke was produced. It was very much an outdoor event, for back alleys and yards, fields, mountains and beaches.

Then somewhere, at some time, some smart oke decides to take a big white Mandrax pill, fold it inside a piece of paper, roll a bottle over it till it is dust, nothing but white powder, and sprinkle a layer across the top of the dagga in the bottleneck and fire it up. This produced a mellow and contented narcotic buzz that became all the rage in Cape Town.

Originally it was just a few urban dopers who took Mandrax pills, eating them like they did in Europe, but it was dangerous because you could just lose it and wander off in a daze and get arrested for being drunk and remember nothing that you did. But a lot of people got over that early stage, built up a resistance and then lived like heroin junkies on Mx.

All over Lucky City the hip cats were smoking it. It was known as the White Pipe, made from tablets called 'buttons' or 'Barry Whites', the big fat pill with the sweet sound of love, the demon that would eat away at the heart of the city. It moved from the suburbs to the streets, into the District and out onto the Flats. People were going mad for it and it became a high-priced item. People were killing for it. They went into the zone and they never came back. I have to admit that I smoked a few white pipes here and there, socially, and did get a little zoned myself, but I stopped after Poison Pete, whose mother was a doctor, told me that the smoke crystallised inside the lungs and was insanely dangerous.

Times were different then. It was the fading of an old world. We had no idea how big it would be, the danger that was coming.

I became known in the Bo-Kaap and by people from the District because I'd been around for so long and was always walking the streets. We all met in the city, on the streets, at the beaches, in the parks and on the mountain. We spent a lot of time outdoors, especially up on Signal Hill, which was like our local park. You could play guitar, drink and smoke without being bothered by the police and then you could saunter down into the city feeling good. Often a walk like that would end up winding through the Bo-Kaap. When people saw me they would say, 'Hey, Luminous, *hoe ga'dit? Waar's jou fokken hoedjie?'* – or something like that.

They were always going on at me to wear a hat. My hair was so light it was almost white, and when a police light shone on me my head lit up like a lighthouse and the *manne* took to calling me Luminous instead of the usual 'whitey' – spoken as a long drawn-out 'waaaaaaaai' like a verbal whip snapping with the 'tie' on the end – the generic insult, to reduce you to your nameless level. Some guys would know you all your life and still never use your real name. Just whitey. So to be called Luminous was more individual, like I had my own name too.

And I got spotted a few times just like they said. Once I was walking with my friend, ou Leonard, from Durban, grooving down the cobblestones, and out of nowhere a police van screeches to a stop and two big cops jump out.

'What the fuck you doing here?' the first boertjie says as he punches me in the stomach and I fall to the ground in pain. 'You are white! You don't belong here.' It was like that. They would jump you for nothing.

Remember that girl before I went to Johannesburg to dodge the army? There was one particular day when we were walking in the Lucky City, me and her. She was young, maybe fifteen going on sixteen, from the suburbs, and the city, my home, the Secret Village, was still a place she had to visit. She was not yet worldly and sophisticated.

It must have been a Saturday morning. In those days everybody went to the city on Saturday mornings and then everything, except the bars, shut down just after lunch. It was a beautiful time to walk down Adderley Street with the throngs of people. We came down through The Avenue, past the Houses of Parliament and the ancient oak trees, starting at the top and walking towards the harbour. As we walked through the crowds many people greeted me. It was not like they knew my name even, though some did, but there were people I'd seen all my life in that city, and these people kept stopping to pass the time of day. Flower sellers, pickpockets, old ladies, young men. So many people. Brown, white, young, old, male, female … and some in between. Some waved. Some nodded. Some stopped to talk. Others touched me, on the arm, the hand with a shake.

After three blocks the girl looked at me with awe. She was at an impressionable age and I had impressed her, this time without even trying.

'All these people,' she said, 'they love you.'

'What?'

'Can't you see? They all know you, and when they see you they smile. It's like you belong to them.'

It's like you belong to them. In the heart of the city, in the village that was built over a stream that ran from the high mountain to the sea, surrounded on all sides by industry and commerce and suburbs, she was telling me: This is your home and these are the people who love you. I laughed out loud at the romanticism of the idea but I secretly hoped that she was right.

HIP CATS AND HOBOS

In the white cities of Cape Town, Durban and Johannesburg a lot of guys thought I was 'cool' and girls thought I was 'handsome' after some media coverage of me as a rock musician was splashed about the cinemas and newspapers when I was just seventeen, back in 1971, and it was hard to shake that image with my peers.

The performance was with the prototype garage punk band Bottleneck, pounding out lyrics to 'Gutbuster' that Johnno wrote: *Wanna be a black man / Wanna have a gat man / Wanna see those white pigs run* ... but we were just one of many that day, playing at what was billed to be 'The First Multi-Racial Pop Festival in South Africa', held at the Green Point soccer stadium. Progressive little town, Cape Town.

What they called 'multi-racial' in apartheid times meant that the pink people would get to sit on the grass in front of the double stages while the more brownish-tinged citizens had to sit in the stands. Between the two hazy shades of race was a noose, a cordon of blue, as a brigade of the South African Police circled the field, making sure no whitey got to meet a brownie. Many of the brown kids brought bottles of Pepsi and Coke with them, liberally mixed with Cape brandy and other exotica. By the time the sun was setting and the bigger-name acts started to play, the bottles were empty and they started throwing them at the police – and those were heavy, dangerous glass bottles, not the little bouncy plastic ones of today.

Anything could have happened, but this wasn't Johannesburg, or Pretoria. Somebody made an arrangement, some genius, and, instead of shooting and killing and being, like, *real downers man*, the police quietly left the arena and the people got together and mingled in a psychedelic love party that spawned many a legend. When they cut the film for the news it was a close-up of me, shirtless, seventeen and god-like in my youth, that stuck in people's memories and I was suddenly elevated, a star of sorts.

I practised my drums at The Office on Long Street, which was an extension of my home. I had spent a lot of my pre-teen years at the swimming pool at the top of the street where it splits into Orange and Kloof Streets. It was our local swimming hole, where all the kids hung around when I was at school.

The Office was just that, an old office in a run-down building with a few dodgy tenants and toilets that didn't work. It was a great location to make noise through the night without being bothered by the police. For a number of years someone in my circle of friends always had control of the place. Some guys even lived there for a while. When you jammed the night away all kinds of people stopped by, made pipes and drank wine or blew their psychedelic minds as the guitars played.

The Office became a mixing place, as we attracted some of the older crowd but also the kids from down the street, Steve and his gang, the Long Street Gang, who weren't a gang in the strict sense of the word. They didn't have tattoos or cause crime. They were young party lords who didn't really give a shit about peace, love and grooviness as long as they could blow their minds.

Steve, when I first met him, was still in school, a year or two behind me at Cape Town High. As a younger guy, he knew of me before I knew of him. He lived a few hundred metres down the road from The Office, above the liquor store in one of the old houses with the metalwork balconies, with his mother and two sisters. His mother worked the night shift at the desk of the White House further down towards the heart of the city. Back then it wasn't socially acceptable to be a single mother. There was a stigma, a stink of shame and failure about it.

They were the only family I ever knew who actually lived on Long Street, which was already attaining a kind of low-class chic with the youth. Hipsters came from the suburbs to Long Street, from the safety of their protected environments to live the quasi-bohemian downtown lifestyle. They opened wild little 'boutiques' and trendy 'art spaces'. Steve's family lived there because it was all they had. Having come from a similar situation myself, I recognised the scenario right away. His mother's house became Party Central and his mom and sisters endured hell as Long Street Steve rocked the house away with crowds of people all weekend long, every weekend.

Meanwhile, up the street, we rocked out at The Office.

For the longest time the Bottleneck crew had consisted of six people. Me on drums and the two Scotsmen, Johnno and Alan, on guitar and bass. Then there was Leonard the Indian guy from Durban who rented rooms above the pawn shop on the other side of Long Street, who was our number-one fan and who always had a bottle of rum, Muhammed who also rented a room there and was our number-two fan, and curly-haired Basil who lived in the District. I think they were all studying together. When we played shows, all six of us fitted in Alan's old Rover 90, the amps and drums in the boot, the three musicians and the guys rolling. One Anglo-Boer, two Scotsmen, an Indian, a Malay and a Hotnot. A jack of rum and a parcel of zol.

We were a hard-driving denim dirt-bag three-piece powerhouse, a little like the MC5, playing some covers but doing a lot of original songs. We weren't a cover band: we were the kind of band that needed to make a record for suburban kids. We first came to light at the big two-night city hall gig in a contest put on by a chewing gum company. All the good drummers were there: the great Anton Fig played on one night and the Mighty Thwaites on the other. Our band didn't win the contest, but we came on with such a pounding intensity that all the guests and stars came out from the dressing rooms and lined the backstage area, rocking out, and Selwyn, the promoter and local music mogul, instantly signed us and gave us twelve well-paying dates out of town. He should have put us in the studio.

It was the wrong fit. We weren't a weekend dance band. Every show we played they paid us off early and told us to leave.

'No wild-man music. We don't do wild-man music,' was the most common remark.

Johnno thought that it was because he wasn't a real singer, mostly just shouting along into the microphone, so he put out an ad that brought us a Canadian singer called El Cid as frontman. We thought it would work, but we were denim and loose sweat and he was kind of mod, all boots and suits. It broke the organic thing we had. El Cid had a few originals too but the experiment wasn't working. Johnno wasn't having fun. Even car space became an issue, now that we were seven people.

The show at the big Green Point festival was the end of the road for Bottleneck. It was a terrible show for us, with Johnno breaking the neck off his baby sunburst Gibson Melody Maker a few songs in, even though he soldiered on with a replacement guitar. The vocals weren't working. The whole dynamic wasn't working.

The day after the festival I just fucked off, depressed about this, that and the whole thing, and disappeared from town. I hit the road, hitch-hiking for the very first time with a two-fisted troublemaker called Mike, heading on my first trip to Durban, where he said I could stay for a while with his family. We stuck out our thumbs through meandering farmlands, dry gravel roads, lush steamy forests, wide open ocean beaches that stretched and stretched, past the pineapple sellers and into the high hills dotted with small villages and cattle, always heading north, till we hit the lush subtropical zone.

I spent Christmas there in Durban but then got in a VW Beetle with Gideon from Springs and drove up to Hillbrow in Joburg for New Year's Eve before spending a few weeks in Springs, sampling the small-town Transvaal life, going from swimming pool to swimming pool, getting wasted in the sun.

Some of Gideon's friends didn't believe him that I was a 'big star' down south until the second week, when we went to see a movie and, before the main feature came on, the news film rolled with coverage of the 'big concert' in Cape Town. While they talked about the event they showed footage of me, movie-theatre size, and blew the local minds. That was the first time I saw the footage myself, so it kind of blew my mind too. I had disappeared from Cape Town the day after the festival without a word to anybody and I hadn't heard a thing about it. After that the word spread and all the kids went to the movies to see me. My bona fides established, the kids and cats were a lot friendlier, with all kinds of invitations to have a good time, but we had to leave and go back to Durban so Gideon could get back to work, and I ended up on the beach at the height of summer. The sand gets so hot in the middle of January that you can't stand on it barefoot.

I was walking with Brian from Bellville with no money in my pocket when the police jumped us and dragged us off to their wagon. We carried no ID and we couldn't prove where we lived, so we were charged with 'Idle and Undesirable'. I was still seventeen, under age, but I told the police I was twenty-one. Just before we went into court, a busy young man with a clipboard told us to plead guilty, otherwise we would be in remand for a month. I didn't understand really, so I said 'Guilty, Your Worship' and was sentenced to forty days' hard labour (or forty rand) in Durban Central Prison, where I got my head shaved and wore the prison-issue 'khakis'. I spent my time in the big old hobo cell above the quartermaster's shop with about forty other men, all the old guys, the gentlemen of the road, the legendary losers.

You learn quick. One minute you are out there being a casual, hang-around, trouble-free joker and next thing you are locked up with all the rituals of confinement. Without committing any crime except maybe being poor and possibly homeless, a person could be stuck in a prison and anything could happen to them and nobody could stop it. It is a hard place to be. Most of the people there have always had a hard time being right in life. You see your own negative emotions magnified hundreds of times in the lives of those perennial losers, tough guys and broken reeds.

It was my first time across the line and into the netherworld of human existence. Everything changes when you are locked up in a real prison. The rules are different. You can't just fuck around. You have to keep your eyes open and your mouth shut. There are complex pecking orders among the inmates and the guards and the right respect has to be shown to the right people at the right times. What's scary is how quickly I adapted to the routines of the prison. After a few days it was all old hat and I fitted right in with the rest of the inmates, looking for tobacco and trying not to get a sharpened spoon shoved into my stomach.

My Indian pal Leonard had finished his studies in Cape Town and returned to Durban. I thought I remembered his address, so I wrote him a letter, asking him to bring me some proper smokes if he was ever in the neighbourhood, because all they gave us was a small ration of dark *twak* we had to smoke in newspaper. That's a fucken taste you don't forget. Twenty-one days into my sentence Leonard showed up and paid the other half of my fine with money he'd borrowed from his sister, and he took me out to stay with his family in Red Hill and meet all of his brothers and his mother and sister. When you walked out their back door there was no yard or garden, just a sloping green and gravel hill that went all the way down to the Umgeni River, where we waded in to above our waists and caught soft-skinned prawns using our shirts as nets, and the brothers just ate them right there. I couldn't do it. Other times we would go down in someone's car in the early morning to fish in the ocean on the Bluff, bringing a whole-loaf bunny chow with the top cut out, made by Leonard's mother.

I kept track of time, and on the day my buddy Brian finished his sentence and was discharged I was waiting outside the prison with a few little things and we made our way back out of the city and down the highways and byways back to Cape Town. It was late summer, a hot journey, and Brian had lost his shoes so I split my sandals with him. He had the left one, I had the right. We ate a lot of mielies from farmer's fields, yellow and sun roasted, and sometimes the potatoes that grew below.

When I got back I found that my drums were still at The Office, which had been taken over by El Cid, who was playing some cool riffs on guitar, and we started jamming towards a new music enterprise with a new man, Deadly Hedley the Guitar King. The Deadly One was older than me, and had caught the music wave with Beatlemania and played in bands wildly with the ravers, the mods and the rockers, and later went psychedelic and tripped out with the first hippies. They had done it all, lived in the forests and done the whole freakout scene. The Older Cats now owned boutiques and had jobs and had moved on from their hippy days, though there were still a few super-relaxed Daddies of Coolness on the scene, not moving quietly into suburbia and other forms of normality. These were the Other Brothers, older hipsters still riding the psychedelic trail occasionally, partying their faces off generally, and mostly just being cool.

7

DIE KIND VAN DIE WIND

The new band was called Buddies, and there were plans to do a small tour of universities around the country, kicking off at the University of the Western Cape and going on to Johannesburg and Pretoria. I went in and did my rehearsal thing, but my heart wasn't in it a lot of the time. I didn't even want to go on tour. But I went for it anyway, after being threatened with a severe beating with a broomstick by El Cid if I even talked about backing out. We were that kind of band. No love, peace and grooviness. No contracts, no recording deal, no money, just a moody, argumentative hard-rocking acid-peak band, four guys who could count to four (and sometimes six), with two guitars, tight riffs and a fistful of original songs written on the Long Street night shift. The week before we left, our bass guitar player Endicott swopped his little diesel Mercedes-Benz for an old VW Kombi, which we christened The Mudshark, and we hit out. I don't know who booked the tour but it all fell apart.

The show at the University of the Western Cape was cancelled and we headed for Johannesburg. During the night we blew three tyres while racing down the highway and the vehicle slid this way and that, the amplifiers and drums crashing around, almost crunching whoever sat in the back. By the time we eventually got to Joburg we had missed all the booked shows, so we played a lunch-time concert at Wits University and then sat, stuck in a house. Who knows where? What a bunch of losers.

I think El Cid had planned to move there anyway so he just went out and got a job in the book business like he had before. Endicott, talented with tools and engines, got a job too. Deadly Hedley and me, we headed out in a van with Zululand Mick, who drove us all the way to Durban and left us somewhere way out in the green hills at a big old mansion, sagging a little, the driveway lined with palm trees, with a swimming pool and bikini-clad hippy girls. Some guy was sitting on the front stairs playing the newish Zeppelin song 'Stairway to Heaven' on his acoustic guitar. The big house was full with those Durban art freaks who made the Polyfilla paintings and sold them at the side of the road, so we stayed fifty metres away down in the old servants' quarters, tiny little rooms with a common stoep, eating avocados, smoking Durban Poison and drinking rum. We set up and hosted some crazy jams there and had some fun with French girls but money was getting tight. Eventually me and the Deadly One, we clashed and he punched me in the head … and broke his hand and couldn't play guitar. There was a girl, or a woman, involved, but that wasn't the reason. I was just a mouthy kid.

After about six weeks I left my drums behind and headed back to Cape Town, thumbing my way down south, sleeping in bushes outside Umtata, curling up in a phone booth in the Knysna forests, enjoying the air outside Mossel Bay and finally drifting back into Cape Town, but I forgot that my mother had moved house, out from the city to Sanddrift, the newly constructed working-class housing estate in Milnerton. Eventually I found my way onto the bridge and across the lagoon to Milnerton beach by the lighthouse, with the mountain blue in the distance, and I met some of the local cats and kids.

But as soon as I could I hit the road again. I loved zipping up and down the coast and often ended up on some strange side journeys with people who knew short cuts. Other times I would walk along wild beaches or farm roads in the middle of nowhere for the hell of it, just because I could. Of course, not all road journeys have perfect endings.

A few months after the Buddies tour, I hiked up through the Free State for a few days to visit El Cid at the house he shared with some Canadians in Hillbrow. On the return trip through the interior I got stuck in the Karoo, the long, hot, dry highway stretching straight and unswerving into shimmering mirages. No water, just me with my harmonica, thirsty and hungry, as all the farmers whipped past me in my sleeveless Union Jack T-shirt. For half a day I just walked.

The world was flat and brown 360 degrees around me, the road a black strip bordered by a low barbed-wire sheep fence on both sides. Sometimes I crossed the fence and knelt down to scoop water from the sheep troughs. Eventually a pickup truck filled with black cats stopped and they squeezed me onto the front seat. This was unusual for me, a black driver picking me up, because there were so few of them and they always appeared to be packed full with no room. Was it the English flag on my shirt? Maybe they needed a white face in the cab to make them look more 'legitimate' for some purpose of their own. The sun was almost gone. Perhaps it was just polite not to leave someone stranded at night.

I sat in the front of the battered old Chevrolet with the three other men. There seemed to be another dozen or so in the back under the canopy. One of the men gave up his front window seat for me, and the driver told me not to lean too hard on the door, as the latch didn't work too well and he didn't want me to fall out. We were as packed as a vehicle can be, way over any legal limit. These men were going to the townships of Cape Town, places like Langa, Nyanga and Guguletu, leaving their families far behind in the interior to work in the city as construction workers, milkmen, drivers and everything else that kept the republic rolling and in business.

I was handed a Coke can, mixed 50/50 with brandy, and we drank while hurtling down the highway. We sang songs and I played the harmonica and eventually I fell asleep until ... holy fuck!

I jerked awake at the sound, some kind of ripping and smashing. I didn't open my eyes. I was deep in my sleep. The noises seemed to go on forever, the sound of metal tearing, and my first thought was that we were still in the mountains that came after the desert. I had a vision of the truck flying off the cliff and plunging down. I knew that I would be dead. I didn't even bother to open my eyes. I accepted my fate and lost consciousness.

But eventually I did open my eyes. Afterwards. Long afterwards. After our pickup truck had crossed the median and the front clipped the oncoming front or side of a huge South African Railways trailer truck coming the opposite way, also a touch too far over the white line. The screeching sound was our vehicle skidding sideways, rubber and metal screaming as bodies pressed against me, forcing the open door, and I flew straight out onto the ground, onto the loose gravel at the side of the road, where I slid, skated, shot for thirty metres on my chest.

I was wearing a tailored Canadian Air Forces overcoat that went down to my knees. They were popular winter wear in Cape Town. The coat was thick, but it was shredded from the top of the shoulders all the way down to the bottom like some Davy Crockett jacket, perfectly shredded as if by the talons of some huge predatory beast.

My face was untouched, my head unscratched. I was unconscious, or stunned ... in a dream. How long was it till the police got there? I lay motionless, crumpled at the side of the road while cars pulled up, blocked by the sideways Chevy pickup and the stationary truck. Eventually the police turned up, laconic, nonchalant, and an officer sauntered over in the night with headlights illuminating my prostrate form.

Some white hippy and a bunch of goddamn blacks.

'*Is hy dood?*' the policeman asked, sounding so bored. People have always driven cars like madmen in South Africa, often with the subtlety of a Cossack troop galloping through a peasant village with no regard for life or limb, and terrifyingly high numbers of traffic fatalities were commonplace to the police out on the Big Road. You would hope, if you were lying broken at the side of the road, that somebody would show some concern, rush over, feel for a pulse, or just put a jacket under your head. You'd hope to hear words like 'Oh my god'.

Everything was suspended. Our truck, my new friends suddenly responsible for the possible death of a white man, the other truck, jack-knifed where it had ground to a halt, the gravel dust a sudden mist in the headlights as more cars were stopped by the accident in the middle of the road. Everybody was looking at my eighteen-year-old body which had hurtled from the sliding vehicle and bodysurfed face down on the gravel and tar.

I was so far from the vehicles that it looked like I had fallen from the sky. There were people, but they stood in a small knot about ten or twelve feet from me.

Is hy dood? Am I dead!? Shit no! Suddenly my mind was there. I opened my eyes and saw lights and spinning colours everywhere. I couldn't remember anything. I thought I must have got drunk and passed out ... I jumped up right away and said, 'No, I'm not dead; *ek lewe nog, meneer*.' But, fuck, there was pain in my arm and blood dripping down my hands.

We were way the fuck out who knows where, and I sank to my knees. Suddenly the spell was broken and people came from the headlights to help me. There seemed to be no ambulance nearby, maybe because it was so late, so eventually one of the motorists offered to drive me to the next town to the police station, where I would wait for an ambulance. They had beautiful leather seats in the back of that Mercedes-Benz, but the old couple didn't seem to mind as I bled out all over the upholstery. My right arm had protected my head as it had slid along the ground and taken a lot of punishment. The pain was intense and nothing moved in my hand.

This fucked everything up. I was trying to make the move from unemployed rock star to professional musician, earning money playing other people's songs in clubs and holiday resorts. My friend Poison Pete had introduced me to a couple of guys with summer residencies booked in the Knysna holiday area but now my hand was ... I didn't know. Pretty fucked up. The old lady in the front seat offered me tea and sandwiches.

They left me in a police station in a small town at about one in the morning, where I sat for over an hour on my own on a spindly old wooden chair, cradling my arm as blood dripped from my smashed elbow into a big pool on the ground till the ambulance finally came and my arm was encased in an inflatable splint by the jolly ambulance driver.

One hundred and thirty painful kilometres later I signed a medical release form to white coats and bright lights and was drugged into blissful unconsciousness and woke up the next morning in Tygerberg Hospital with my arm in a cast, a smashed elbow and a shattered wrist (multiple fracture of the right epicondyl). There goes the bloody athletics career! The doctor told me that I shouldn't think of playing any musical instrument professionally because 'that is some serious damage'.

It was another whole trip in that hospital, where all the pretty Afrikaner nurses fawned over me, calling me '*die kind van die wind*', their velvet bell-bottomed child of the highway who came flying out of the desert in a truck full of black men and lay twisted on the side of the road.

All the familiar stereotypes reared their heads and met the usual friends and foes. I ended up in a room where the other occupant was a policeman with a lower spine problem who couldn't move from his bed. He didn't like me at all. It was his job to hate long-haired communist hippy rock 'n' roll drug-addict kaffir-lovers. He was a smart cop and he knew what was going on.

There was a brown cat who swept the floors and did other janitorial work and every afternoon he would give me a little flick of the head and a few minutes later I would leave my bed, put on a gown, and follow him around the corner and out into a courtyard under a tree where he would produce a bottle of see-through and a big fat zol.

The cop knew exactly what was going on and he seethed with hatred. To make things even worse, his wife and teenage daughter came to visit him every day and their hearts just melted when they saw me with no family or friends, and they took to bringing me all kinds of presents and sweet treats to eat. It drove the cop demented. They were so cute and clean. I even told them that they didn't have to bring me food, but they didn't listen to me or him. They would swish in and out in their lovely wrinkle-free frocks, doing as they pleased. I had a few naughty thoughts about that playful young *vrou* and her perfectly coiffed daughter with the sweet pink lips.

After a few weeks I couldn't take being cooped up with the angry policeman any longer and I slipped out of the hospital in the middle of the night and hitch-hiked to the city. The first place I went was Long Street, to The Office, where I picked up the sticks and began to practise with the plaster cast on, determined to recover and not to submit to those dread predictions.

Eventually I had the cast removed and practised hard, five hours a day, but it was already different and I played differently because my wrist didn't bend like it used to and for a long while my elbow didn't straighten properly.

My hand and arm were back in action though, and I learnt new and unconventional stick control techniques with my fingers to make up for the lack of mobility. Playing the drums is not like playing other instruments. With a guitar or a piano, the instrument has to be in tune and then any two notes played together at the right intervals make a chord. The drummer, on the other hand, has to tune his body, like an athlete. The more you work the more fluid you get, and the more fluid you get the more in tune you are with the song.

Even though my body would bear a few permanent reminders of my accident, I was confident that it would be usable again, but while my physical self seemed to have some ability to recover from sudden violent trauma, my mind was a whole other story. It was caught up in some strange place. I was here, I was there. Hot and cold. Darkness

THE UNEXPLODED BOER

came in the night time and in the morning. All emotions were rendered unto the grey dream, the colourless, bleak gothic landscape of suicidal ideation.

★ ★ ★ ★ ★ ★ ★ ★ ★ ★ ★ ★ ★ **8** ★ ★ ★ ★ ★ ★ ★ ★ ★ ★ ★ ★ ★

THE PSYCH WARD

I think that being fucked up, unhappy in the most basic and fundamental sense, gave me a better and truer vision of my homeland. Because I was a naturalised immigrant, a patriotic citizen of the United Universe of Unhappiness, I could see it everywhere. I could stand on Signal Hill and feel it radiating from out there in the distance where the sun rose.

I never thought about that first assault by the paedophile, or the others that happened from when I was twelve to fourteen. I told no one, not a single person. I just blanked the events out of my life, and pushed the memories away into some corner of my mind. It was only years later, when I was on LSD one night, maybe eighteen years old, tripping in The Office on Long Street on my own, wailing away on El Cid's old stripped-down Fender Mustang with immaculate screaming feedback through that old Fender Bassman amplifier ... one summer night, playing like Jimi Hendrix and tripping out on Window Pane or Green Goblin. I shifted my vision to the left just a little.

I think it was the left, anyway, and it's like there was a wall, a glass wall that I had never noticed, and on the other side was a parallel world to the one that I was living in, the depressed, cynical, draft-dodging, under-employed, hard-practising musician that I was trying to be, and I looked a little closer, drawn to the figures that seemed so familiar, my nightmare memories that had been hiding right in front of me all those years, and then the partition just disappeared. No grand explosion, no rent in the space-time fabric. Suddenly I saw, I remembered, my sexual initiation, the disgusting man-and-boy filth that I had so cleverly hidden from myself. There they were in front of my eyes. Just like that.

I went into some kind of panic mode. My body was ice-cold, encased in a sheet of frozen shock. It was the strangest thing, but when I saw that pile of shit sitting there in my head, I realised that I had always known it was there. There was no sudden revelation, but I felt more complete. I wasn't living in the dream of a lie, a self-deception, any more. I just never talked to anybody. I kept the secret from others and from myself. I think we all do have the choice not to see. It is a survival trick to save us from going mad.

The other thing that can save us is people.

I was in total shock from what had just happened, the guitar hanging silent around my neck as my mood took a nosedive from high to low, and suddenly there was this booming sound in the distance – *bang, bang, bang!* – echoing through the dark corridors outside The Office. Someone was down on the street, kicking the door to get my attention. It was the Secret Knock known only to the Other Brothers and the Long Street Gang. I was still in my LSD panic attack, my breathing shallow, my body out of my control. I had never had a panic attack before.

Out of habit I put down the guitar and went to answer the door. When I opened it I was relieved to see that it was the Charlie-Bird's brother Eddy, a brother of great standing, a cool daddy from way back who was well connected to the Other Brothers, a soul man of eloquent disposition and good humour.

Eddy had The Power. He was so beautiful, talking in that languid intergalactic Ultrafornia drawl that has no region, no country. He was surrounded by the most beautiful colours, around his body a pinkish glowing aura, and he suggested that we go out, stroll up to the Metropole Hotel and grab a couple of ice-cold Carling Black Labels.

Until then I hadn't ever been a drinker, a *juice-head*, and the idea of sitting in a bar while tripping had never occurred to me, but Eddy was so cool, so calming, and we strolled in the hot night and, I'm telling you, that cold beer was the best thing I had ever tasted. I relaxed and all the panic, the bad energy, just flew away. Yes, the bad memories were still there, but they were already just memories of bad memories. But old Eddy, what a cat, he just shows up, out of the blue like that, and smoothes me out one time.

After that night, I was on a campaign to expose all things hidden. I was tired of evasions and lies and half-truths and wanted to be real for once. Unfortunately, the panic attack that had accompanied the knowledge was not a one-off event.

I started to have repeated attacks of anxiety. They could come on anywhere, while I was sitting and smoking a pipe in a back alley, or in the middle of a conversation with an old friend. Often, after entering a room full of people, I found it impossible to leave, as I became frozen on the spot. Other times I would be strolling down Long Street and just the sight of an acquaintance would trigger an attack and I'd turn around and walk out of the city, way up the slopes of the mountain where there were no people. I spent more and more time alone on the mountain and on Signal Hill, reading and writing and staying away from people except when I was jamming with the guys at The Office. Even then I would have attacks in the middle of a song, but I just endured it and tried to weather the storm.

I did drop acid once or twice more but very quickly found that the experience turned into nothing but hours of torture, because I would get psychedelic anxiety attacks. I had truly lost my cool and felt like a walking lie. The only thing that helped me integrate socially was alcohol. When I drank, the feelings of terror were subdued and I started self-medicating more and more, but I couldn't get drunk. I didn't stagger around and do stupid things. On the contrary, the alcohol made me feel calm and centred.

Not understanding the nature of anxiety, I came to the conclusion that I was losing my mind and had gone mad. It was, after all, in my genes. When I was a boy I was told the story that my Boer grandfather had had a psychotic episode and had shot a nun in the leg. He had spent almost a decade in Valkenberg mental hospital, that austere colonial gothic monstrosity built in 1891 and situated in the Cape Town suburb of Observatory, standing on a vast lawn between the Liesbeek and Black Rivers. As a very small child I had often seen it in the distance on trips from Fish Hoek to Cape Town, although back then I had no idea that my grandfather was locked away inside. Later, as a teenager, I would see it every other weekend when travelling to play away games with the Cape Town High School hockey team. Like Robben Island, it was a notable landmark of fear and mystery.

I knew someone else who went there: my friend Harry, the beautiful and gentle musician with a sweet bluesy voice and equally natural talents on the saxophone, guitar and keyboards, had been confined there, apparently as a catatonic schizophrenic. Harry was older than me, and had played in the sixties with the legendary Four Jacks and a Jill, and was a member of the avant-garde group Abstract Truth and the psychedelic powerhouse Freedom's Children, as well as many other notable bands. I first got to know him as a shuffling mute who never uttered a word, during my hard-rock psychedelic heyday with Buddies.

Often during the all-night jams someone would go downstairs for some fresh air and Harry would be standing there, his nose pressed against the door with an irresistible smile on his pixie-like face surrounded by a black mass of Marc Bolan curls. He would shuffle up the stairs and stand wordlessly in one place for hours, stretching out his hand for his turn when the bottleneck pipe was being passed around. In those days I only saw him talk once. One of the band members had just received a thousand hits of acid from his friend, the Fat Man, in

London and everybody got one – including Harry. The LSD was fresh and strong and one by one the musicians put down their instruments and sank to the floor, powerless and wordless in the grip of the multi-coloured trip. But Harry, he became animated and started talking.

'Hey, is it all right if I play your guitar?' he asked, receiving mute assent from El Cid, and then he went to the microphone and sang a haunting version of 'Sometimes I Feel Like a Motherless Child' and went on to play a complex building drum solo on my drums, followed by a bass guitar solo *à la* Charlie Mingus, and finally made some sweet, sweet sounds on the Charlie-Bird's saxophone that brought tears to my eyes. As the peak of the drug wore off he once again subsided into silence as the rest of us regained our ability to move and speak.

The trouble with Harry was that he had a penchant for jumping out of windows. I don't think it was a suicide thing. Once, when his speech had returned after many series of electroshock treatments at Valkenberg, he told me that he had been a giant bumble bee. He didn't like the treatments and often ran away, only to be returned by his brother-in-law Jack (some said for the rumoured twenty-five-rand reward), who would often walk proudly around town with Harry's empty guitar case stencilled with the names of the famous bands he had been in.

Unfortunately, a few years later Harry's mother moved to the tenth floor of a building in Durban and Harry became the bumble bee again while visiting or staying with her, and took one final flight from which he never returned.

But that happened much later.

I had lost my faith in my mother's God to ever do any good in my life. I decided to cross the road and go to the doctors. I wanted to get treated and fixed up by these great men of science who had the whole game figured out.

I convinced myself that I was a paranoid schizophrenic, mainly because that was one of the few mental health labels that I knew of.

Armed with this knowledge I went to Groote Schuur Hospital, up to F3, the psych ward, and asked to speak to a doctor. This was highly unusual, I found out, but eventually a doctor agreed to talk to me. I told him that I believed I was a paranoid schizophrenic and would like some shock treatments to help the pain go away.

To his credit, the doctor didn't burst out laughing in my face, but it was probably the first time anyone had walked through the doors of F3 and demanded The Shock.

'I really need shock treatments to stop the madness in my head,' I pleaded. This was me at my most rock-bottom desperate, because I had never pleaded for help before or asked for anything from anybody.

'That's not the way it works, my boy,' the tolerant doctor informed me. 'To come into this ward you first need a psychiatrist who would evaluate and treat you and, if he thought it necessary, refer you to us for hospitalisation.'

I left the hospital feeling more depressed than when I'd arrived. There was no way I could afford high-priced luxuries like psychiatrists, and I still had no idea that what I really needed was a psychotherapist, someone who did more than dole out pharmaceuticals. Even though I had the lifelong habit of keeping things inside me, I really needed to talk. I was ripe; I was open for communication and cure. I made my way back to my mother's little house at Sanddrift.

My problems were compounded by the arrival of my first military call-up papers, giving me a date to report to the Cape Town Castle to do my duty. I needed to get a job, earn some money and leave the country. I desperately wished that I had parents who could just send me off to Berklee College of Music in Boston or the Kenny Clarke-Dante Agostini Drum School in Paris, but I already knew that wishes didn't work. I had tried to get jobs here and there, but without much success. Hell, I had even gone and taken the long aptitude test to work for the South African Railways, where any idiot could get a job, but was informed that I'd scored 'too high', intelligence apparently being an indicator that the employee would move on to something else after a short time, thus wasting all their training.

THE PSYCH WARD

I had to make a plan. I had to use the phone number and call Tricky Dick.

I had first become aware of Tricky Dick when I was about sixteen and he followed me home, tailing me in his car like a private detective, up Orange Street all the way to my house, but, unlike a sleuth, he was easy to spot because he was driving a Rolls-Royce Silver Cloud, one of the most obvious symbols of affluence at the time. Then, insulated by the superior arrogance of money, the *droit de seigneur* of the capitalist, he had the audacity to knock on our front door and ask my mother if he could speak to me.

My mother was quite impressed and she called me excitedly. 'There's a man out there in a Rolls-Royce who wants to speak to you.'

'No! You must be crazy. He's a homo,' I told her. 'They are always following me.' So she went out to his car and told him that I would not be coming out.

Over the next couple of years I had spotted him spotting me here and there and I always made a point of dodging away, except for the last time. It was one of the final anxiety-ridden acid trips that I had taken and I was hitch-hiking with Sailor Dave, one of Long Street Steve's close pals, on the road to Green Point, heading for some night spot with pumping music. The Sailor was out of control, letting his mind flow free in the wind, and I had just dragged him out of the road where he was endangering his life pretending to be a traffic cop and directing cars like an orchestra conductor, when Tricky Dick pulled up in his Rolls.

'Hi boys, are you looking for a ride?' he asked in an insinuating fey drawl.

Before I could say anything, Davey-boy says, 'Oh yeah, man,' and jumps in the back seat, so I followed suit.

'If you boys want a drink of scotch, just open the cabinet in front of you and help yourself,' the Trickster offered. In a short while the car had changed direction and we were cruising the highway drinking Johnnie Walker Black Label with Elton John cranked up on the stereo,

THE UNEXPLODED BOER

on the way to Tricky Dick's house in Wynberg. He was really showing off, and, as we went around the corner on De Waal Drive, he activated the air compressor which boosted the suspension, and simply drove off the road onto the side of the mountain, driving across the grassy plain and through the trees while screaming at the top of his voice – 'Weeeeya!' – and eventually made his way back to the road. We were impressed.

We ended up sipping Tanqueray and tonics out of giant cut-crystal goblets in the Trickster's brand-new house, tastefully decorated as a show home with expensive furniture, the walls covered in antique mirrors and the swimming pool artfully lit by discreet lighting. Everything was immaculate. After a few drinks he figured out that we were definitely not 'pick-up boys' and no sex action was going to take place, especially when Sailor Dave asked to use his bathroom and took a big dump in the bidet. Finally we were driven back to the city and dropped off on Lower Long Street, which had become known as a night-time cruising area for male prostitutes. Before he left he slipped me his business card and told me if I ever wanted a job I must just give him a call.

The time had come to make the call.

It turned out that Tricky Dick ran a landscape-gardening company, the bulk of his business devoted to the gardens of wealthier people around the Wynberg and Constantia areas. He was like a high-class hairdresser, very in vogue, as much for his garden design talents as for his outrageous flamboyance, even turning up to shovel manure out of the boot of his Rolls. It was the early seventies. David Bowie and Elton John ruled the pop charts and gay chic was very much the reigning style. Camp was high, and my employer Tricky Dick was in fact the high-camp queen of Cape Town, as he drove around in his silver Rolls with his two borzoi hounds, both dyed silver to match his own platinum hair. The cat must have been at least six foot tall and wore huge diamond rings, high platform shoes and the widest silk bell-bottoms imported from France.

We all had our looks at the time. We all wore our uniforms. I had a frank talk with him right up front. I wanted a job that would pay me some money. He said he had an opening for a trainee in the garden management and design and creation business, with lots of hard labour, digging holes, shovelling soil and manure, moving rocks, and digging more holes.

'I just need work,' I told him. 'I want to learn and make money but ... you do know, I'm not into the man thing.'

'Yes, tiger,' he cooed. 'You've made that quite plain. I am looking for someone to teach the business to, someone I can delegate responsibility to eventually. I can get my fucking sex whenever I need it. Don't you worry about me. So ... when can you start?'

Staying in Sanddrift and not having a car, there was no way I could feasibly make the daily commute out to Wynberg to work, so we came up with an arrangement. He met me in the city late on a Sunday night and drove me to his place, and I stayed in my own room, complete with four-poster bed and drapes, during the week, and spent my leisure time in the evening drinking gin with duchesses and hobnobbing with the decadent elite who talked of mansions in Spain and apartments in New York. Tricky was, in his way, trying to help me by introducing me to 'society', giving me a step up from the same gutter he'd clawed his way out of after dropping out of high school. On Fridays he would drive me back to the city, where I would resume normal life with my girlfriend and rehearse with my band.

I suppose he thought I would eventually come round and become his partner, totally ignoring the fact that I had a girlfriend. Men – gay or not – can be pretty thick in their sexual aspirations. Other than that he was a cool cat, but he had all these schemes that he was working on, planning to open a cordon bleu restaurant, and, in his fantasy, I would work there for three years and then become a partner in the business and so on. It was quite amazing, because really the only thing keeping me sane was the Tanqueray gin. Truth is, if he had wanted, Tricky Dick could have beaten me up, raped me, drugged me, whatever he felt like, because behind all the queenly posing and all the 'daahling' talk he was tough and he was big. But he was a nice guy, so he didn't.

On the weekends I went home and tried to save my money, but sometimes I would get so depressed that I would set fire to the bills, watching them burn, and then hurl all the coins into the bushes.

I was earning less than I'd got for my very first job as an assistant lighting technician at the Nico Malan Theatre, but I lived 'free' from Monday to Friday, drinking like a fish and eating like a king ... or queen. I drank a lot of gin and ate caviar and baby pheasant. Tricky wanted to buy me expensive clothes and jewellery and stuff like that, but I refused all gifts. He said he'd buy me a sports car – very tempting to a young guy – but he admitted that this came with strings and I reminded him that we had been through this at the beginning.

The guy was victim to his own loneliness and it was easy to figure out that other people had taken advantage of him and grabbed what they could, cruising off with their little sports cars and new wardrobes. I didn't mind being paraded about with the crème de la crème, the beautiful people, who all liked me because they were older and I was young, and they made assumptions about our relationship that were not true. I was tempted to take the gifts and have all those new fancy Italian shoes, but it just felt wrong.

Eventually Tricky compromised and gave me what I needed instead of what he wanted. After finally hearing what I was saying about my state of mind, he set me up with a rather dull psychiatrist – and that's when I found out that a psychiatrist is just another kind of drug dealer and no use to me at all, so, to impress on this Medical Man the severity of the situation inside my head, I took all the drugs at once one weekend. After that he didn't give me any more, but arranged for me to go to the psych ward F3 in Groote Schuur.

So now, instead of going from home to work every week, I went to the F3 ward, returning home on the weekends. Institutions are comforting at times, because they are like God. They take care of all the bigger questions and provide you with food and shelter. I was hoping, in my therapy fantasy, to get the intuitive Jewish psychiatrist with the gold-framed glasses who sat on the couch laughing and making jokes with the suicide girls, but instead I got the other one, Dr Van der Merwe. They thought, probably because I had an Afrikaner surname, that I should be paired up with a stodgy, recalcitrant and ineffectual Boer shrink. In South Africa at the time, they would tell Van der Merwe jokes (just like in Canada they tell 'Newfie' jokes and in Amsterdam they tell Belgian jokes). Now I had my own personal Van der Merwe joke.

For two months I was in the F3 ward, hanging with wrist slashers, pill poppers and those who never came back from Flip City, and the nurses injected me twice a day with tryptanol to chill me out and I went to group therapy every day. I loved it. After that night when my cursed memories had come back to walk with me in the sunlight like my prodigal doppelgänger, all I wanted was to expose all the lies and seek the truth whatever the cost. Unfortunately, all the other patients in F3 wanted to hide everything and mostly wanted to die. I told the good Dr Van der Merwe about my new memories, hoping in vain for some feedback, but he never told me a thing or gave me any diagnosis. Not a single word of feedback. It was like telling my darkest secrets to a potato.

Of course it wasn't all therapy and drugs in the old F3 ward. We had a lot of time to ourselves in the afternoon and I soon found that I could slip out of the ward, take a wheelchair and trundle down to Main Road in Observatory to the liquor shop to buy some booze. Word soon got around among the patients and I was besieged with requests for alcohol. Being pretty much broke I saw a good opportunity, and agreed to buy it for them but demanded double the going rate and made a killing. I'd wheel down to the shop and return loaded with bottles of vodka, cane spirits, brandy and gin. This sideline came to an end when one of the nurses spotted me tootling around outside in my wheels and reported me. I was told that I had to stay 'on ward at all times' and a watchful eye was kept on me from that day on.

Eventually they had a big day where the patients were called in one by one by the Big Boss of psychiatry, Professor You-know-who, who sat in this special room raised up like a king, at the top of a grandstand of seats. Spread out below him were the Lords, the various doctors all in a row, and below them were two rows of nursing staff in their clean white uniforms. He just asked me one question.

'How long have you been a practising homosexual?'

That was it. My hesitant attempts to talk about the after-effects of the paedophile attacks were interpreted as confessions that I was a tortured homosexual afraid to 'come out'. No doubt the professor, being very hip and avant-garde, felt that outing me in front of all these people would break the secret and make me feel better. It's what they wanted to believe. Everybody was coming out of the closet in those days. Nothing was cooler than camp. Even Mick Jagger was kissing Lou Reed in public. Because a gay man was paying my bills it was automatically assumed that I was his bitch.

All that time wasted. Those idiots knew nothing. This man knew nothing about me. To him I was probably just a clinical file, a piece of data to be used as a reference in some grand paper on the Sexual Habits of Left-Handed Drummers. That Big Boss professor of psychology, I knew a lot more about him than he knew about me after two months of observation. I'd gone all the way through high school with his gregarious daughter who was much loved by us all, who wore her breakdowns on the outside. I knew that her grandparents had been 'bohemians' who lived in Paris, hanging in Montmartre with the artists and poets, wearing nothing but sackcloth, back when it counted. He was a number-one hip shrink. I was there when his daughter crashed and burned on black bomb speeder pills during the big exams and just wrote the same words over and over. As a schoolboy, I'd been to his fancy flat at Clifton Beach and had a beer with his wife who was sunbathing topless on the balcony.

Tears welled up in my eyes at the knowledge that I had wasted my time and that psychiatrists were not going to be of any help. I shook my head from side to side. 'I think, never,' I muttered and I left the room.

It hadn't been a complete waste of time. While I was in the F3 ward my military service date was almost due and the doctor, Van der Potato, had written to them and got me a four-month reprieve. I'd hoped he would tell them I was mentally unfit for the army, but hey, them's the breaks.

That night I sneaked out of F3 and didn't return. I went back to work with Tricky Dick, but after a few days he finally felt compelled to make his move on me, attempting to touch me while I was sleeping, crossing the border of no return, and I gathered my things together at three in the morning, walked out into the night and never went back there either.

9

SHOULD I STAY OR SHOULD I GO?

My need to escape from the military became even more urgent when I saw what happened to Long Street Steve. Like all white boys, Steve had to go to the army and, even though I had spent long hours waving my Mathematical Wand of Explanation, he still went and did his military service up on the border of Angola in the adjacent annexed country of South West Africa … where I was born.

When he came back he had these big neck and shoulder muscles and looked a bit like Popeye the Sailor Man, and he would tell stories, explaining how you go crazy when you've been tracking a 'terrorist' all day long in the bush – about how, when you get to him, already killed by the first soldiers on the scene, you see that he was just a barefoot youth with a piece of shit gun, and you line up with all the guys, screaming and emptying your clip into the dead body, all of you, the whole squad, in a killing frenzy, as the nameless child's body jumps and jerks and little bits break up and fly in the air.

The killing, he left it behind in the desert, but some of the madness followed him home, I think. His life seemed to have become one long drinking binge, and he did things that went over the line into murky areas. One time, walking up Long Street in a group late on a Sunday night, money gone, sobriety approaching and without thinking, as we passed one of the many private liquor shops he just jammed his elbow sideways and shattered the giant plate-glass window, reaching in through the falling shards, taking two bottles and running, followed quickly by the three other guys, two bottles each, so I grabbed a bottle and ran after them up to Steve's house, but in the end I didn't drink with them. It didn't feel right. I left the bottle and went home.

He was discovered by the *manne* in the Bo-Kaap, where he spent more and more of his time, as it was the nearest neighbourhood, across the road and up the hill. Over time he became a linguist, and collected new words and idioms of the local Cape Afrikaans patois. It seemed that he had lost all interest in making it in 'white society', the smiling Euro-gloss veneer painted on the reality of life. Increasingly he gravitated to the Bo-Kaap.

I got the idea that he didn't like white people that much, that he wanted to disappear into the townships or up into the Bo-Kaap, but just like the people in the townships who wished to be university professors, doctors and politicians, poor Steve was held in check by that two-way cultural constipation of apartheid. He was sentenced, by law, to live with the boring whites in their segregated toilet of fear. I think that Steve was hunting for the Secret Village. I always suspected that he had more than two eyes.

It is safe to say that there were always areas where a white boy couldn't and shouldn't go, especially in the Dark Days, but Steve went anywhere and everywhere and so the greater city discovered him and his endearing fearlessness. To say simply that he was a linguist is wrong. He was a master, a wizard of the Taal. I saw him myself, when we walked in the Bo-Kaap late at night, back from dinner at 'Tiema's, or with a *borrel see-through* and some *stoppe* from the Wale Street merchant, when a gang of *skelms*, as was their territorial privilege, would sidle out of the darkness and onto the old cobblestones, fanning out like gunslingers.

If they knew me they'd say the usual, 'Hey, Luminous, *waar's jou fokken hoedjie?*'

But just because they knew me, it didn't give Steve an automatic pass. They didn't know him … yet.

'Jy, waaaai-tie, give me a *dop* there *ek sê.*'

He wasn't a tall guy, old Stevie, and he would stand there looking up at those gangsters with their beautiful almond-shaped eyes of death, his little woollen *hoedjie* pulled down low on his brow, and he would let loose his tongue. He could do things with insults that were truly beautiful, and not once did I see a knife pulled on him. It wasn't what he said, but more how he said it. No, it was deeper than that, more than how he spoke. It was the way he cradled each and every word, like they were precious. If he could have made multicoloured bubbles come from his ears it wouldn't have been as entrancing. He gave them these words of his, the things he treasured most in the world. He was irresistible once he started, pulling phrases and stretching them like a magician and tying them into knots and rolling them across the road like a soccer ball with the unspoken challenge – can you kick it back?

How could they resist? It was one thing to have someone in your territory pay his taxes in blood, but to be challenged to a poetic duel in your own language, it was a whole different league. A *waaitie* walking Browntown in the night was always going to be challenged, sometimes on every block, but Steve won them over every time with his sheer courage, his honesty and the purest stream of verbal abuse in the city. He was a street poet, a rapper, truly the Ou Z, the original zef master.

Perhaps when your own people desert you, you are free to choose for yourself, and so Steve, in search of people, of belonging, of a story to which he could attach himself, chose the home team. He didn't choose the overlay, the *lanieskap*, the pretty carpet of Eurocentric civilisation that had rolled across the City of Luck. He chose instead the underlay, the Kullid world, as his world, as his people, as his language, as his culture. If there was an immigration office he would have lined up and got his papers.

Maybe it was the army that did it. Before he went in, I used to tell him to save up, to go away, not to do their dirty work for them. He just shook his head.

'Where would I go?' he would say. 'There's nowhere else in the world that I want to be. I have to do this if I want to stay here.'

'What about your father? I know it's none of my business, but wasn't he a sailor from Norway or something?'

He looked at me straight. 'I come from here and there is nowhere else I want to be. I don't want to go be a star in Joburg like you. I don't want to go to England or California or fucking Norway. I like it here.'

For me, living in South Africa, things were clammy with dirt. I was always putting everything off and constantly feeling afraid of the police and wondering when they would get me. I knew so many English people and somehow I got the idea that I just had to get to London and everything would be okay. It would all be civilised and I could get a job and go to university and play music and live happily ever after.

After my job with Tricky Dick, I was still in the country without much hope of leaving. It was nobody's fault, just me and my stupid head. I hadn't been totally slack though, and had acquired a valid passport and an international vaccination document, plus I had put down a deposit and bought a new set of Yamaha drums, so I did do a lot more practising because I was at home, living in my mother's yard at the side of the house in a four-wheel Gypsey caravan.

I took a few days and hiked up the coast to Durban to see if my old mushroom drums were still where I'd left them at the mansion, but they had been stolen and only the cymbals were left. I sold them to another guy and went straight back down to Cape Town because my girlfriend's parents had just offered me the job in their butcher's shop outfit, the family biz.

I worked hard at the butcher's shop and practised hard, getting a few funny little gigs playing cover songs in the sailors' clubs downtown. I moved from the caravan in my mother's yard to an old house back in the city, tucked away at the end of Rus in Urbe Avenue, which I shared with Harry and a bunch of other people until my army papers came again. That's when I took off on the train to Johannesburg with my drums and ended up staying in the house in Parktown North with Endicott, El Cid, the Joker, Granola Boy and the super-delicious QT, the Queen of Mayfair.

QT and her bosom-buddy, the outrageous Contessa Carol, took me through the night haunts in their city. We were always so blasted that I don't remember much. Cape Town's rocking son Louis Greef from Omega Ltd was there playing a residency in one of the clubs, knocking them dead with his guitar, but the big sensation was keyboard whiz Duncan Mackay playing at the Branch Office where all the musicians would gather to blow their minds.

I was always getting side-tracked. I had hoped to make some money in Joburg but I wasn't very successful in that department, and I got into the band thing, rehearsing and playing gigs, but it was going nowhere. When I received my third set of army papers I knew that very soon there would be some military police making enquiries on the streets around my mother's house.

The same old solution always came up: leave the country, leave Africa, get the fuck away and find a life. But first I quickly had to become a criminal.

10

TAKE THE MONEY AND RUN

The apartheid version of life in South Africa was attractive to many people around the world and they flocked to the country. One of these people was the Joker, the wannabe drummer from England who lived in the front room of the house in Parktown North, a guy always on the hustle. I didn't like him at all and he didn't like me, but we were such opposites that we were somehow fascinated with each other, and in the course of conversations he became aware of my army predicament and offered to help me out. (More likely he saw a way to use me to his advantage, I saw later.)

When my mother sent my third set of army papers to me in Johannesburg I was freaked. I went here and there trying to find some kind of job but I was already flying so far on the outside of normality. It wasn't like I could just go down to the labour bureau and get a job sweeping the streets or digging on a construction site. All those jobs were reserved for black people. I was supposed to put on a suit and tie and do something … sociable … and … it wasn't the most social period of my life. A lot of people got jobs through their family. My family had no jobs.

The Joker, now, he really wanted to be a drummer. The only problem was that he really could not play and wasn't willing to put in the time that it required to at least keep a beat straight. The Joker had other talents though. He had arrived from England like so many – a descendant of a long line of working-class yobbos, peasants, vassals and foot soldiers – only to find that in South Africa he could be the boss.

He could strut around and call people names and preen and pose and the whole damn place was set up for him to do it. It was a con man's paradise. All that he had been raised to be, a peasant worker for the rich, was reserved for black folks only; in South Africa he could be the *guv'nor*, the *squire*.

The Joker was in sales and used his mouth to make money. He always seemed to be driving someone else's Mercedes-Benz. He was good at talking but he was a master at shouting. He particularly liked abusing the black lady who was the 'maid' in the house where I lived. He did it on purpose: gloating at the way other South Africans squirmed, people who didn't want to face the abusive underbelly of their lives.

He would stand at the back door in his platform boots and his too-tight crotch-hugging bell-bottom trousers and scream across the yard. 'Heeeey. Heeeeey! Where's my goddamn laundry? Come oooon! Fucking Jesus Christ!'

When she arrived to do his bidding, he carried on, abusing, shouting, bullying. 'Come on! Cuuuuum oooon!! What the hell is it with you people! You never do what I tell you!' He'd follow her and harangue her from close behind, mere feet away from her ears, like a verbal jackhammer.

The lady was used to that kind of asshole and she just brushed him off. I got to be friends with her boyfriend Samson, a man of about fifty. We'd sit in the backyard drinking tall beers and smoking the odd fat zol. Old Samson was a painter/contractor who earned more from a week's work than the Joker made in a month, and on top of it he seemed to come and go with impunity, ignoring the pass laws and curfew restrictions that the Evil Empire used to control the black population. Of course I only knew the tip of that man's mountain.

The Joburgers didn't quite get the idea of me sitting in the back drinking tea and consorting with the black folks. To me, it was natural, because it was exactly what I had done in the Cape, not as an overt attempt to communicate with the 'natives' or anything so demeaning. It was just people, and we talked about life, about beer and about how stupid our beautiful country was. I did tell Samson about my problems with the army and vowed never to pick up the gun for 'them', and I was rewarded with many an ice-cold Lion Lager for my pains.

I was really just a bum, because I didn't have a job, and I hung around with QT, the rock 'n' roll queen from Mayfair who lived in that house in Parktown North, and I played in a band with two guys who had jobs and I found my own ways to get food and money. QT worked in a cigarette factory, so every week she would bring hundreds of free cigarettes for the house. Samson showed me an overgrown and disused vegetable garden in the backyard and I ate from the earth. But, still, I was a bum and I hated it.

The Joker said he knew a man who liked to help young fellows of army age to leave the country, so one night he took me to visit his friend, whipping through the dark Johannesburg streets in yet another flashy little Mercedes speedster.

It was a wealthy neighbourhood, a beautiful house filled with beautiful things, and I wondered if I was just another purchase to be added to the collection. Who was this mysterious benefactor? From my young point of view he was a flabby old man, maybe fifty-five or sixty, some sad Fat Fuck. He had inherited a company that was a major supplier of medical equipment in South Africa and he didn't need to strive too energetically for his daily bread. Materially he had everything he needed. Spiritually ... that was another story.

We had been drinking before we got to his place, but the side effect of the heightened anxiety that ruled my nervous system had kicked in: I had absorbed huge amounts of alcohol but wasn't getting drunk. The booze just dulled the pain, but many co-drinkers thought of me

THE UNEXPLODED BOER

as a major party animal because of my tolerance and stamina. We sat on the couch in the man's opulent living room, knocking back scotch faster than they could make it, while the Joker wove his slimy web of words.

He played the man. He wheedled and cajoled and whined and begged as we descended into a maudlin alcoholic stupor, the corners of the room growing bright with scotch-induced flashback flares. On the other side of the room was a large display cabinet filled with dozens of beautiful Buddha statuettes, fat ones and skinny ones from diverse parts of Asia. I seem to remember that in the middle of this all the Fat Fuck produced a chequebook and wrote us some loot.

It was a strange situation, slipping into the warm amber tones of scotch whisky, the comfortable couches, the smell of expensive fabrics, and the Joker strutting up and down like some little curly-haired Napoleon in platform boots, holding his cigarette like a dictator, hurling words, spitting abuse and acting like the biggest shit on the planet. It was a bizarre tableau. As the Joker got more arrogant, the Fat Fuck became more compliant, apologetic, subservient. It was a complex ritual dance that I had not witnessed at the Saturday twist sessions we used to go to at the Green Point soccer club.

We drank still more, knocking it back like water. The Joker kept working him, accepting cheques and then, a few minutes later, laughing and ripping them up, hurling the pieces back in his face, papering the carpet with torn-up cheques, and raised the ante, again and again. Finally the Joker left the room with this guy, and I carried on drinking alone. It was then that I committed the crime, and even while doing it I felt the burning shame of corruption on my soul. I opened the display cabinet and took one of the Buddha statuettes for myself, not one of the fat ones, but a skinny one, a Cambodian with the pointy thing on his head. Then the Joker returned and told me to go and see the man in his room.

So Jokes was my homosexual pimp. Is this how he made his living? Is this how he made his contacts and got his Mercedes-Benzes, by trading his youth to the appetites of the elderly? Isn't that what film stars, magazine models and porn actors do too, with varying degrees of conscious complicity? Is it good or bad? I don't know the answer to that question. I just know that it has existed since time immemorial. The brief flicker of youth is a commodity traded eternally.

I went into the bedroom and he was lying naked on the bed, on his stomach; a white, fleshy, sobbing mess. It was pathetic. He was pathetic. I didn't know what to do. What was I supposed to do? What had the Joker been doing in the room with the man? I knew that I wasn't going to abuse him in any way, even though it was apparent that that was what he craved. I just sat there and watched the man cry, his flesh bobbing and heaving with the sobs that wracked his unhappy life.

Too many times in the preceding years I had got jobs only to find out that the 'employment' hinged on an understanding that I would become sexually involved with the man, often married. I never lucked onto women business owners who wanted to engage me in carnal action. I had no real marketable skills except that I was alive and breathing. It just seemed that the only people who ever wanted to give me a chance were these men – but it is not a real helping hand if you have to sell yourself. That is not what I call a friend. That is what I call an eater of souls. So 'fuck you' I spat at those shitheads!

But was it really their fault? There was a game and there were rules. I was just too marked to play the game with the boys or the girls.

I looked at the sad Fat Fuck on the bed and I wanted to kill him, but he was so pathetic lying there crying. Waiting. Waiting for what? What did these men do? Was I supposed to fuck him up the arse or masturbate in his eyes? I needed the money. I didn't want to kill anyone with the Gun of Authority. I didn't want to spread even more misery for the Paedophiles of Power. The nightmare of my adolescence was my vampire cloak. Punk rock was born from this world, creating the need to destroy everything in a blind nihilistic rage. The devil calls to us day and night. You only have to sell yourself once to be useless forever.

I wanted to beat him to death with his metal Buddhas, his expensive collection, his stolen loot. Who was he to think that just because he had bought the Buddha he could buy me too? Is that what money does to people? Does it make them blind and stupid? It was the perfect time for murder – the drunken twisted youth and the old Fat Fuck, blood spattered on the walls and the mirrors. Blood on my hands and my face.

There was one thing wrong though. It was in the smell or the aura or some indefinable sense not yet categorised by science. I knew he wasn't a pervert, because he didn't have the smell, the taste. The Joker was a hundred times filthier than that poor slob. Once you have smelled the filth, it never leaves the nose, the back of the throat, and that poor unhappy man didn't have it.

While he sobbed in shame or hurt, out there in the darkness somewhere a South African policeman was torturing someone in every city that night, kicking handcuffed men in the head, throwing them out of buildings, all to keep this rich man safe. But still he was not happy. All over the country, people were hungry for food, thirsty for water and shivering in cold tin shacks, but the poor slob had no idea that he could have been a nice man. He could have helped someone without expecting them to whore in return. I couldn't kill him though, because he was just another victim of the perverts.

I staggered out of the room and said nothing to the Joker about what had happened. He said nothing to me either. We smoked another cigarette and drank more scotch and then left with our cheques and took them to the bank, waiting in the dawn until it opened, smoking endless cigarettes and pacing back and forth, and we got our filthy money with the booze still coursing in our veins.

The Joker was good though. Man, was he good. After being awake all night drinking, we were still pretty wired. He got me going and told me that the party wasn't over yet, so we rushed to the airport and bought two tickets to Durban, stopping only in the swankiest shopping district, where I bought myself an off-the-rack French-made black velvet bell-bottomed suit lined with satin, and stumbled onto an aeroplane. We drank more scotch on the flight and when we arrived in Durban, where the bananas grew by the warm Indian Ocean, we jumped into the latest Mercedes-Benz that the Joker had hired for us and sped off to the fanciest, tallest skyscraper hotel down on the beach.

As we drove up, men in hotel uniforms came running down the palatial stairs to take our baggage, but I opened the door and vomited all over their shiny black shoes. Embarrassed, the Joker roared off and we returned a few hours later with less fanfare to take up our residence in the top-floor suite. Needless to say, the Joker managed to get me to part with my share of the money as easily as he had persuaded the Fat Fuck to give it to us. He almost succeeded in making a total fool of me, showing me how he could talk up thousands of rands in a moment and then, poof, it's all gone on Monday morning. When it was all over I woke up back in Johannesburg with a headache, a velvet suit and, miraculously, a return air ticket to London that I must have bought at some point on the drunken spending spree.

A few weeks later, as the deadline for my ticket approached, I realised the futility of trying to get to England with no money. There was a minimum requirement of four hundred rand and a return ticket for entry as a tourist into the United Kingdom. Four hundred rand was a lot of money, although I had spent almost that much on my suit. The Joker, on the other hand, had not purchased an overpriced suit or a plane ticket, so he went out and bought a huge brand-new Ludwig 'Vistalite' drum set which dominated the music room.

He was really pissed off at me too.

The Fat Fuck discovered that the Buddha had escaped from his glass case and he wanted it back. The Joker told me he knew I had it and I should give it back and all would be forgotten. Thing is ... when we were partying like the Rolling Stones in that hotel in Durban, I had gone out in the pre-dawn light and walked barefoot past the homeless people sleeping in the bushes and across the smooth cool sand and onto one of the wooden piers jutting out into the Indian Ocean, and, as the first golden glimmer approached on the horizon, I took the Buddha and threw him high, flipping end over end into the sky, till he entered the water with a tiny silver splash.

    The last time I saw the Buddha he was executing a perfect backstroke, moving smoothly and with ease, happy to be free in the morning sun, but sad too as he headed north-east in the direction of Cambodia. He was going home. He had a different land to heal.

THE PLAN

I cancelled the ticket to Heathrow, took the money and hitch-hiked to Durban to see a contact of my friend Surfer Nick, an old lady in a small village outside the city, who made a living from selling Durban Poison, the best weed in the land. I decided to use my knowledge of the country to make enough money to get away and start a new life.

I would become a smuggler.

It was the only way I could think of to make money without the government knowing. I knew where the product was and all I had to do was make the journey there and back a few times and I would be set. Ready to go. It was no big thing. In fact, the total cash involved in the end was so pitifully small as to warrant words like *pathetic* or ... *loser*, but I wasn't in it for the profit per se; I didn't actually *want* the money. I thought it was a venture I could just drop in on, extract the minimum amount of profit and then go far away.

I was a stupid dreamer.

I arrived in Durban and booked into the faded yellow Springbok Hotel, an ancient and discreet establishment tucked away in the shadows of the skyscraper hotels. I contacted Surfer Nick and he took me out to Big Mama's place, driving out on the highway towards Pietermaritzburg until we got to a specific petrol station, where we parked the car. We walked about a kilometre further to an almost indistinguishable footpath, which we then followed up and down for about an hour until we arrived at a collection of rough dwellings.

It was a shanty village, a community peopled with old men, children and women. The men – the husbands, fathers and grown sons – were all away on contract, digging in the holes of Johannesburg for the gold or coal or whatever the industrial needs dictated.

There were kids on the outskirts of the settlement and they came running to us, grabbing The Surfer by his hands and dancing around singing, 'Hey Nicky, Nicky, hey Nicky.' We were led to Big Mama's hut after 'Nicky' had his cigarette pack almost emptied by the kids. The lady lived up to her name. She was indeed very large, with multiple layers of chins and a multicoloured *doek* wound around her head. She dealt with us from the comfort of an ancient red armchair that looked at least a hundred years old.

The Surfer spoke to the lady in a pidgin of Zulu and Afrikaans with a few English words thrown in, introducing me as a good friend. Then he told me to show her my money. I laid the cash out on the tea-box table and she counted it and then pushed it back towards me. Putting two fingers in her mouth, she issued a sharp loud whistle, which brought a boy of about twelve running to the door. She gave him instructions and he spun around and raced off. While waiting for the boy to return we were offered hot sweet tea followed by a shot each of very high-proof home-made liquor I knew as *gavin* or *gavien*, a rocket fuel that burned the throat, warmed the stomach and set my nose running all at once.

I was still trying to douse the flame in my stomach with tea when the boy returned with a brown-paper bag which he handed to Big Mama, who emptied it on the floor at her feet and counted out the neatly packed rolls of Poison for me to see. Each roll was made up of twenty pencil-sized sticks wrapped in paper, all combining to fill the air with a familiar delicious peppery smell. I nodded, she nodded and we made the exchange of money for goods, then she reached under her armchair and pulled out an extra roll of twenty, tossing it at The Surfer with a wink and a smile.

THE PLAN

I had memorised the way, because the next time I would do it on my own. The fewer people involved the better.

Once I had The Stuff, the big sweat took over. Carrying a Stash is not fun. It is all hyperventilating and stress.

I had spent all my money on this investment, so I had to hitch-hike the 1600 kilometres to Cape Town carrying a rucksack full of dagga – in a police state, where often the only people on the roads at night were police – down through the Transkei to Port Elizabeth and along the coast through the Knysna forests and on to Mossel Bay and the final run through the mountain to Lucky City.

I ate bread and drank milk and I slept under the stars as always.

I had hitched rides up and down that coast many times, but this was the first time I was carrying contraband, something that would interest both policemen and thieves, so I wrapped each roll carefully in tin foil and then in plastic to stop the product from drying out but especially to prevent any odour from leaking out.

My first ride out of Durbs was with a travelling salesman in a Peugeot 404, which always happened on my road trips. I often wondered if there was some rulebook that said all salesmen had to drive the same car, but they were generally nice and friendly, especially if you weren't a bum. They were just looking for company and conversation so they didn't fall asleep and drive off the road.

I was dropped outside Umtata in the middle of the afternoon and there I hit the doldrums. Nobody would stop and, as the afternoon wore on, I was thinking of going to find a place to eat and then make camp somewhere nearby when finally a big transport rig loaded with cars pulled up in a skidding cloud of gravel dust. The driver said he was heading for Port Elizabeth. I didn't have to worry about him smelling my rucksack of Durban Poison, because his cab reeked of freshly smoked weed.

'So, you look like a turned-on hip cat,' he said to me, eyeing my star-spangled T-shirt. 'Do you skyf?'

'Well, ja, of course,' I replied with a smile, and he pulled a Mills cigarette tin from his pocket, flipped the lid, and offered me one of the many pre-rolled joints from within. I took one and lit it up, offering it to him after a few puffs, but he lit his own.

'*Jislaaik*, no man. I'm not from Durban, I'm from the Cape, and the rule down there is always "one man, one *pil*". You start from the beginning and you take it to the end. A man has got to have standards. You know what I mean?'

'I am from the Cape too and I give you no argument about that,' I replied, 'but I thank you very much for your hospitality.'

As the night darkened he kept on smoking and joking until I started falling asleep and he pulled into a petrol station to refill his coffee thermos.

'You look like you need a *dos*,' he said when he returned, 'so why don't you climb into one of the cars and stretch out on the back seat and I'll wake you when we hit PE – and, here, take one more zol with you, my *bra*, 'cause we gonna ride nonstop through the night.'

I took my bag and the joint and climbed into the car nearest the front, because I didn't want to spend the night bouncing up and down with the cars further back. I had done this before. I was still half asleep and dazed when he jumped up and let me off in the early hours of the morning in Port Elizabeth, shoving two more joints in my hand 'for the road'.

'No, man, I can't. You've given me too much already.'

'Hey, don't insult me, my *boet*. I got plenty more where that came from,' he laughed and jumped back in the truck, which roared off in a cloud of smoke and dust. I had to walk quite a way through the city to get to a good hiking spot on the other side, where I soon caught another ride. It seemed luck was on my side as the rides came quickly and, even though some were very short, I made it to Lucky City safely and in record time.

Once I got back home I stayed with Long Street Steve and the boys at Dobbs's house, the Beatle Headquarters near Buitenkant Street. Now I had to sell the stuff.

I was going a little further underground, into the black market. This is where things overlap. Drugs. It was the newly fashionable time of the drug culture, and many young pirates played games, selling drugs and making money under the table. Young businessmen. The lifestyle could be good, especially in a police state. When the laws are harsh the profit margin soars. Some people got kicks out of playing games with the bumbling undercover police goons trying to be hip infiltrators, and I heard many a tale of adventurers who took pride in their mental prowess, testing their wits in a secret-agent fantasy. I wasn't one of those players. I wasn't a real drug dealer. I was just impersonating one to get some quick money.

Before this criminal venture I smoked weed because I was a Cape Town Roker Boy and that was a good thing to be. I had done a bit of Mandrax, and I'd taken a fair amount of LSD but stopped after I realised what a crappy time I was having. That was the extent of my life of crime and drugs: public enemy number four million, three hundred and seventy-two thousand, two hundred and fifty-three in the hierarchy of evil. Boring.

As usual, I was a terrible salesman. I just hated doing it and relied on a few friends telling their friends. Business was not as brisk as it could have been and I was buying too many bottles of tequila and Southern Comfort. Also, I know that Steve, bless his mischievous little heart, was stealing up into the attic and purloining some of my stock. Needless to say, profits took a bit of a hit, cutting into the funds for my exit strategy Master Plan.

Luckily my old friend Poison Pete stepped in to help. He was a perplexing guy who I'd known for quite a while. His mother had arrived in South Africa as a teenager with her grandmother after the Second World War, their Eastern European village taken to Nazi death camps, their family entirely exterminated. Poison Pete had dabbled in drug dealing since his mid-teens in high school. I don't think he needed the money, but he played that game, and seemed to collect interesting and beautiful people, always managing to be in the know and at the show.

I got the idea, already at that age, that I was only seeing one small facet of Poison Pete. It seemed that he had always been around, in some way or other, and even though he came from the Other Side of Lion's Head, very much part of the *lanieskap*, the Happy White People, he inspired in me a total trust. I always thought that he was one of the Good Ones.

Poison Pete made me a Capitalist Proposition, in which he would go to some friends and raise money, selling the stuff ahead of time, so I would have more money to invest. I thought it was a capital idea. I moved my game 'upscale' a bit, because the hitch-hiking was too nerve-wracking, and went to Durban by train instead. When I got there I would register in the Springbok Hotel as usual until I had made the purchase.

As soon as I came back with the stuff, I changed out of my nondescript clothes and became a Rock 'n' Roll Queen, donning my black velvet suit, silver Indian earrings, satin shirt and bright white takkies (*no socks required*), and signed into the big posh beachfront hotel, my white leather suitcase packed with Poison. I'd stay one night, take a taxi to the airport and fly straight home.

★★★★★★★★★★  12 ★★★★★★★★★★

POISON RUNS

I did the run to Big Mama's Poison Palace half a dozen times over a period of ten months. The village was a couple of hours by car from Durban, in the rolling hills. I would turn up there and put in my order. There were kids 'keeping eyes' all over the place, watching the rough gravel back road that wound over the hills, the opposite direction from the path I took, for *polies kar*. Usually I would have to wait for twenty minutes to an hour while a runner was dispatched to get the goodies from the Secret Hiding Place.

The village was a collection of fifteen or twenty tin shacks. Shantytown. I was used to it. I hadn't grown up in it and I was lucky, I suppose, being on the other side of the colour line, and getting electricity in the wall and water from the taps. But I had been all over, and, in urban areas in those days, when you weren't in white man's land you were mostly in shantytown, with corrugated iron and bare floors and newspapers and magazines as wallpaper.

I would wait with the old men, too old to work, as they sat in the hot afternoons drinking home-made beer. They would allow me to sit with them, after all the bullshit that was brought on their lives by the blue-eyed people – they would seat me in the circle, offer me beer and let me be there.

When they drank too much they would try to dance. Old Zulu warriors jumping in the air and stamping the dry gravel dust. They wanted me to dance, but I knew nothing of their culture. I was from the Cape, so far away from the serious Africa vibe, a culture where the men had forgotten how to dance together. Technically you are of Africa, but on the edge of it, like Alexandria in the north. But I jumped in the air and stamped my foot on the gravel for them, because there were no other young men for them to impress, and they were the only senior citizens I ever sat with, besides my grandmother. The beer was good too.

But, when the kid returned with the dope and the time came to make the transaction, it was a tense business. I could be a cop for all they knew. Or the boere could be over the next hill. I was stressed, they were wary, but with every venture there is a point that you have to cross. The tough part. Making the deal was definitely one of the tough parts. Flash the Cash.

They could arrive shooting, beating with clubs or biting with dogs. People could be dragged off screaming, wounded, dying, and have their skulls brutally booted against the police van. White man in black area was against the law and highly suspicious. I was a dangerous commodity, but I brought money. *Geld.*

The third time I went there, when the kid came carrying the stuff and I walked towards Big Mama's house with the money, all of a sudden there was a flurry of communication.

'*Boere,*' hissed the little boy at me. '*Polies.*'

He shoved the big sack of Durban Poison sticks in my hand.

'*Hardloop,* run!'

So I ran. In one hand I had the money and in the other hand I had the *gunston* and I took off in an adrenalin rush of fear and just kept down and moving and away for hours until it was almost dark. Then I realised that I was ahead of the game. I had the money *and* the stuff.

I could have just taken off, but instead I went back, because I just didn't have that killer instinct. Call me young, colour me stupid, but in my head there was always this imagined abacus upon which

I played a game called the Mathematics of Honesty, my personal mixture of superstition and pop-culture karma all rolled into one mess. Also there were those feelings, the sudden knowing: right or wrong?

I know that a lot of people in the world have the 'finders keepers' philosophy, or 'you snooze you lose'. Some people pride themselves on getting ahead at the expense of 'stupid' people. I think I must be one of those stupids. I had all the money and the weed and I was miles away, down by the highway. I just had to make a phone call from the petrol station phone box and I would be picked up. They would never find me, never see me again. I could leave, go away, bye-bye Africa. Instead I went back, very carefully, creeping through the undergrowth like a commando until I finally spied the shacks, peaceful in the dusk. No cars. No vans. No police.

When I appeared, the kids all laughed at me. *False alarm!* They fell about as one boy mimed me jumping over bushes and trees. But when I went into Big Mama's hut with the weed and the money to pay her, I swear she looked at me a little differently. She reached under her chair and pulled out a couple more big fat rolls of Poison and tossed them in my bag and smiled.

'Bonsela,' she said, and after that it was different, because they remembered me as *the one who ran away but came back with the money*. After that she always gave me more than I could pay for. My first credit account.

'Jy sal later betaal,' she said in one of my languages, because I could not speak hers. She trusted me.

Life was looking up. After my third or fourth Poison run, early 1975, I ended up back in Cape Town with an actual place to live, paying rent and sharing a house high up on the slopes of the mountain between Oranjezicht and Kloof Nek with four women: Bridget, Jay, a mysterious redheaded Swiss girl with snow-white skin and silver snake jewellery, and another young woman whose name also escapes me, but she was overly endowed by nature and liked to share with the world by removing her bikini top on Clifton Beach. A guy remembers things like that, especially because it attracted about fifty guys at once. I thought I had it made, Mister Cool, living in a house with a bevy of sexy independent women.

I knew Bridget from before. She was the daughter of a World War II Spitfire pilot. A good girl. A bad girl. On the surface she was a bad girl in every way possible. She was not the most traditionally beautiful or the most vivaciously stacked, but she was economically and athletically streamlined, with no waste, no excess, except in her volcano-like energy. Gifted with an irresistible drive, she radiated vitality, energy, purpose, an electric dynamo driving her, perhaps driving her crazy. She had the blood of a Boadicea, a warrior woman, but she parked her chariot in all the wrong places.

She was just a fifteen-year-old schoolgirl whose father owned a cardboard-box factory when I'd met her two years before in Milnerton, out along the beach towards Blouberg, dressed in her blue school uniform with that gang of carefree kids, mostly first-generation settlers whose parents had English accents. Happy White People with their jolling and their cars and swimming pools and maids and braais and gardens and gardeners to tend to them. Okay, I am laying it on a bit one-sided. They also had bad days, suicide and sadness, problem children and alcoholic relatives, but in the grand scheme of things, they had a pretty damn good life as they operated on the fun side of the economic spectrum. And they really *were* wonderful and loveable people.

Even at that young age, Bridget was working up a head of steam and seemed to have the goal of fucking everybody worth fucking, and a lot who weren't. She was a total *skandaal*, in fact. The second time I met her she stripped naked in front of me, her best friend's boyfriend, and casually put on her bikini with an evil smile. I got the idea right then that, if you let her, she would collect your testicles and keep them in a jar in a cave somewhere. After I left the Cape and moved all over the country I only heard bits of gossip about Bridget, even from my older brother, who had dated her briefly, and her reputation as a Bad Girl was growing. Just the way she planned.

When we shared the house at the mountain, Bridget was pouting because I had never 'made it' with her, plus she thought I was wasting my life away. Actually, she never pouted, she wasn't the pouting kind; she seethed with unconcealed anger. She thought I should be fucking rich girls and driving Porsches and hustling my way to the top.

I had only one plan, and that was to get the hell out of the country by doing my Poison runs and making some money. That whole *smokkelaar* thing I did reluctantly, as a terrible necessity, not to amass large amounts of money and do the criminal jol. There were lots of people doing that sort of thing and Bridget ran with them, the hotshots with brains, the bad boys with guts and egos. She liked the high flyers and the power players. I think she thought I was finally showing some initiative by engaging in crime and she didn't really believe me when I said I was going away.

I had been saying it for so long.

Every night after midnight, Bridget's lover would come – a tall, well-built black dude called George, a shadow in the night, slipping into the house. I don't think it was political with her; she was just trying to be a bad girl and stick her finger in the eye of the world. In that time of Grand Apartheid, it was the greatest taboo, white girls fucking black men. It was also a crime, the minimum sentence being nine months in prison for the first 'offence'.

We all lived there in the heart of the Lucky City, right up against Table Mountain, me and four wild women (when I wasn't on the road) with a stash of Durban Poison and an endless bottle of Jack Daniel's on the midnight run to sunrise. When you live there up against the mountain like some tiny bug, it is not the same as in the tourist pictures, the panorama of Table Mountain spread out before you. The rock face towers up, like an enormous granite wave, frozen forever as it rises before crashing down to clean the earth and start again.

★★★★★★★★★★ **13** ★★★★★★★★★★

THE LAST TRIP

I prepared for another run. This was to be my Last Trip. All I had to do was get rid of the stuff and leave the country and live far away from all the pain and the lies, my family, my country, my sad little heart.

Just call me Jonah!

That last time I did not take the train. I drove instead with my old drummer friend Donny, who was taking a holiday, a cruise up the coast and then inland to Joburg to see his good old pal, Derek the Taxi Driver. I should have stayed in Durban, turned around and gone home, but it seemed logical to make a run to Egoli, say goodbye to a few people before going to Europe, maximise my profits, then return to Durban, reinvest and fly home and leave the country. I didn't like being a criminal or a sales guy. I was afraid.

I had never included Johannesburg on my run before. It was a big and dangerous city that didn't tolerate fools. While Cape Town had skollies, Johannesburg had tsotsis and gangsters and men of gold. Everyone was a hustler, a player. It wasn't my turf and I didn't have enough contacts there.

I should have known better.

Endicott's brother was supposed to be some kind of part-time drug dealer in the Bronx (Hillbrow) and, along with his roommate, he was going to take the stuff off my hands, so I figured I would go round the corner to the liquor store, skollie-style, and begin drinking brandy sometime in the afternoon while waiting for the guys to come over. Donny took off to do some other stuff – that hard-core drinking wasn't for him – and I sat suiping on my own in the winter sun under the peach trees in the backyard.

There may have been vibes. People thought I should just settle down and get a job, and they ignored the whole thing about the army and 'the system'. They predicted that I would go to Europe and come back with my tail between my legs, spouting the usual 'I fucked up in Europe' story, and then I would settle down, so why waste all that time? Wake up and smell the coffee, boy!

But I wanted to move on, to make a start. All the time I had a panicky, anxious feeling that life was slipping away, slipping through my fingers. I was twenty years old and dying to do something. I should have already been in university for a few years, like the other kids from my class. I had no mentor, advisor or benefactor. Mostly it was my responsibility, but I was incapable of asking for help. I didn't know how.

I mean, people could agree on some stuff but it was just too big. The government was just too big. Everything was messed up, even my family – the Afrikaners on one side and the English on the other. Two solitudes with a long bitter relationship and then the Afrikaners with their dispossessed brown cousins living in shantytowns and the massive black majority relegated to the crumbs, punished brutally, worse than animals, for even thinking.

All these bad relationships, this alienation, the lies from the British Empire, the mad nightmares of apartheid, everyone callously ripping out hearts and trampling on the Living Dream. I knew I had to leave. It was too big for me. I drank the brandy on my own in the cold sunny backyard, and when Endicott's brother still hadn't turned up I got tired and went to the garage that used to be the music room and found a spot where I dissolved into dreamland, the sleep of the stupid and the drunk … on the night before The End of My Life.

And while I slept some idiot covered me in wood.

Even aces get shot down (their little bodies hit the dirt)
Some reputation earns a crown (ja, some angel lost his shirt)
Even aces get shot down (even champion swimmers drown)
Babies, I would be your champion
If it would help you stand your ground

CHORUS: but don't play with me – you know I can't resist
please don't play – I'm all that I've got left
please if it's a game – you know your life's at stake
so please don't play – I'm all that's left to take

Even aces get shot down (by other aces don't you know)
That's the only way (those flying champions go)
Vainly fighting for control (his 'chute is shot to shreds)
The picture fades, the page is turned …
You wake up safe in bed.

14

JOHN VORSTER SQUARE

John Vorster Square was named after Balthazar Johannes Vorster, who sat in power as prime minister of South Africa during the psychedelic years, the Golden Age of Rock 'n' Roll, from 1966 to 1978. He was not a groovy dude. His enduring legacy, this giant police station complex, was already full of hate and sadness during his time in office. Motherfucker was still ruling while I was in his shitbox, the house of 'law and order' where criminals were dragged and deposited for fingerprinting and charging and photographing, and held for trial for days or weeks or months or till they died.

John Vorster Square: where the police did the bidding of the government and incarcerated and tortured and killed political dissenters month after month, year after year, bodies flying from the tenth floor to the deadly ground below. All the way down there in Cape Town, even with the self-censoring media and the big smug quiet, I had heard about this Lubyanka, this Bastille of Johannesburg, from university students. Big city. Big men. Big trouble.

As we drove through the streets of Johannesburg I sat silently, withdrawn into myself, trying hopelessly to readjust to the shock of the situation. I knew about John Vorster Square, with the arrogant all-knowing assumptions of youth, but I didn't even know where it was. I was really just a tourist in Johannesburg and had never had any occasion to seek out the infamous SAP base, so it came as a surprise to me when we didn't park in front of a police station charge office but instead turned into a discreet industrial back entrance and began our descent into the dark caverns of an underground parking lot.

As the sunlight disappeared through the rear window, the big cop, the one who seemed to be running things, turned in the passenger seat and faced me with a smug smile.

'My name is Detective Sergeant Boetman,' he said, 'and this,' he indicated to the other cop, 'is the Jew.' He said this with such gusto, such relish, knowing exactly the effect it had, how his subordinate co-worker was positioned. Humbled in front of criminals. With my social conditioning, where it was the law to insult black and brown people but a terrible thing to insult a Jewish person, I was shocked myself. But the other cop, the Jew, he didn't flinch. He played along like it was a compliment. Maybe it was.

The police car went deeper underground into the many garages under John Vorster Square, where fleets of armoured vehicles awaited the coming revolution, ready to take the people on. Boetman leered at me, fully aware that he held all the cards. I was the type who paid the price for all of his unhappy school days.

'Welcome to my world,' he said.

It sounds cheesy, but that's the way he talked. At that time, Clint Eastwood's character Dirty Harry was a big role model for goons, and it showed. (Clint, you asshole, you should have quit after the cowboy movies and gone straight into producing and directing. Hundreds of thousands of thugs worldwide felt validated by that fuckhead Harry Callahan and his stupid oversized Smith & Wesson revolver.)

After parking, the policemen pushed me through the concrete gloom to the dull-brown lift doors and Boetman spoke to me again.

'So you play in bands, hey? Are you a singer?'

'No, I play the drums.'

'Well, you are going to sing,' he promised sardonically as he shoved me into the lift. 'We are going to teach you how to sing, aren't we, Jew Boy?'

I didn't answer him. What could I say? I had already lost the battle. Conversation seemed pointless, serving only to make me more depressed. The lift went up and up, and when we emerged from it we were many floors above the ground, in what could have passed for the offices of an insurance company: all paperwork, desks and cubicles, bustling with men in shirtsleeves going about their seemingly mundane clerical work. Here I was fingerprinted and photographed and humiliated and dragged through all of the initiation rituals by various officers.

While I was in their custody I told the fingerprint guy that I really needed to go to the toilet, and he sighed like it was a big problem but escorted me and waited outside. I really did have to go and quickly relieved myself, but I also used the opportunity to remove my earrings and flush them away, because I had heard nasty stories about other guys having their ear lobes ripped open during interrogations.

Once I had been fully processed I was handed back to Boetman, who took me into one of the rooms. There must have been twelve men sitting there in cheap shiny chairs. *Was this some kind of party, or a training session?* I was ... how do you explain, after your world has toppled over and you're left wondering about the who and the what and the when and – worst of all – the now? And what about the future?

There was all this question bullshit. Sometimes there was goading and hitting. I kept my eyes down and played stupid. Didn't have to do much pretending. I was very naive. I mean, if I was a *playah*, a real secret agent, I would have been formulating some way out of that Palace of Doom, cutting a deal, any kind of deal, perhaps promising things I could never deliver. But I didn't.

At one point a man came in who they called the Colonel. He seemed to be the big man on the floor. The Colonel stormed into the questioning room, seething with barely controlled rage, and pointed his finger at me while shouting, 'I want you to break this one quick, he's a disgrace!' Then he strode down the hallway back to his office.

THE UNEXPLODED BOER

Boetman told me that they had been tailing me in downtown Johannesburg and lost me the day before in rush-hour traffic and that they had a *shoot to stop* order out on me. He mocked me and told me nobody was going to care about me in prison. Were they following me before I went to Endicott's brother's flat? Did I lead them to him? Why had they been following me? Boetman showed me albums with hundreds and hundreds of photos, mugshots of all the guys he had put in prison. Then he showed me the photo of the only one who got away.

'The only one – but I'll get him one day.' He laughed at me. 'Guys like you, you look for me. I just sit and wait. We knew about you before you even left Cape Town. There was no way you could have got away. *You* were looking for us.' Was any of this true? If they knew about me before then …?

That gave me lots to think about. How people fell like dominoes. Who did what? Who did what? Was there anybody to be trusted … anyone, anyone? All weekend thinking: Who traded me? And why? For safety, for revenge, just for money? How many people in a row all traded little bits of me, selling my freedom for … I wonder what? I wonder who? Or were the police just making it up, playing with my brain, using some standard method of demoralisation? Who in Cape Town? The people who gave me their money? Poison Pete, who raised my venture capital? Hardly anyone knew what I was doing and even fewer knew what kind of vehicle I was in and who I was with on this trip.

It's the real world. This is what happens when the players play. Forget all those theories and lectures, hippies and songs, promises and wishes…

'They are all gone now,' Boetman jeered. 'Where are your friends now? I can promise you you won't be seeing them again. You are the last person they want to see. They don't care about you. Nobody cares about you in here. It is just stupid to be "loyal" and protect them. They wouldn't do it for you.'

He was right. I could see he believed it was true. His world was the world of truth, the world where people broke, and broke down. His was the place where people traded their friends, their enemies, and their families – anything for freedom and another chance – and he was the breaker. That's the way a police state functions: corrupting and destroying the souls of the young and creating the desperate and sick zombies they call citizens.

But then, sometime during that long day – or maybe it was the next day, I don't remember – who should stroll through the door but my good friend Endicott. I don't know how he tracked me down, but he just wandered in with a couple of packs of smokes for me and struck up a friendly and deferential conversation with the authorities. They talked happily about me in the third person as I sat there, dejected. Endicott joked with the cops that he too used to be a silly young man but emphasised how he had seen the light and changed and was *a good citizen with nothing but respect for the police and the rule of law.*

It was a strange conversation. I didn't tell the police that I'd sold Endicott a couple of rolls of Poison just a few days before and that he had them, forty beautiful brown-paper-wrapped, hand-rolled, sensimilla Durban Poison sticks of the finest blend on the continent, stashed under the doghouse, the kennel, outside to the left as you walked out of the kitchen. *I would never tell them that. He was my friend and I was from the Cape and we keep the circle tight.* We don't betray our brothers. I never saw Endicott again.

While I was being questioned I saw various hippies, guys I had seen out there 'on the scene', walking in and out of offices and past our little room. Were all those guys plainclothes policemen or were they people who had been turned and were reporting in and informing on their neighbours and co-workers just to stay out of jail and to hold on to their jobs and keep their records clean? Were they reporting on me?

What was really happening out there on the streets?

I was exhausted. The day had started with a brandy hangover and seemed to go on and on, reverberating forever like those dead afternoon mirages that stop time in the hottest days of summer. Luckily I had the cigarettes to clamp my jaws on, because I was offered no food or drink, though the cops sometimes left for refreshments themselves. The hardest part was waiting to go to the toilet, imagining how much fun they would have making me soil my clothes if I asked to go, so I just kept my mouth shut and my guts clenched.

When Boetman finally got tired of ruining my life for the day, I was put in the custody of the Jew, who handcuffed me again and took me back downstairs and out through a discreet side door and shepherded me from the police office building to the big prison building, the actual 'police station'.

It was my first view of John Vorster Square, situated at number one Commissioner Street, and it was intimidating and awe-inspiring just because of the sheer size of it. I stared up at the six-storey blue-tinted concrete monstrosity, at the expansive front stairs more suited to a university or a place of public gathering than a palace of oppression, and just before going through the glass doors I twisted around to look at the building where I had just spent the worst day of my life, the ten floors of offices where the questions were asked. I know now that I was 'lucky' to be dealing with third-floor people, the drug squad, because, dangerous as they were, they still adhered to some rules. The higher you went, the worse it got, with the top floors reserved for BOSS – the infamous Bureau of State Security – and their torture devices.

It was so casual, so blasé, the moustachioed goofballs. They were used to treating people like rubbish, used to breaking human beings down with threats and power, blackmail and pain. Breaking them till they were nothing. Making people do things for which they would hate themselves forever.

Those who did not debase themselves were thrown out of windows or sent down, down into the pits of doom. Now I don't equate myself with those poor people, the ones who were tortured and thrown to their deaths, the lost heroes of the Struggle to Be Free, but

I was there in that same place, in some ways for the same reason. We were all victimised by the state.

In the prison building I was once again stripped and humiliated and finally put into the cells where the vultures waited for new meat, for cigarettes or money or any fucking thing, their hands clawing, feeling, talking their own eager language, their eyes roving, searching your body for whatever treasure the police had left you with. Customs agents on the borders of hell. (Ever been to sea, Billy?)

I had a bit of money. The police had taken my bag of cash and stolen most of it, leaving me with about forty rand, a bribe to say nothing about their theft of evidence from me, plus I had some cigarettes. Cigarettes were thirty-five cents a pack back then and a brandy and Coke cost about nineteen cents in a bar, so forty bucks could still go quite far. There were seven other people in the cramped cell, all wanting to be my friend, and I shared my smokes with them.

This was institutionalisation at its worst, not organised like a real prison with schedules and goals and so on. It was a temporary detention centre where drag queens and dope smokers were in with murderers and psychos. Violence was the currency. From the moment you were brought in to the men's holding area, the cops violated and demeaned you with violence and screaming. In the cells too there was always the threat, the chance of violence, with so many unstable and desperate men all together, some disorientated, others experienced and giddy with anticipation.

This was apartheid, and apartheid reached even here, so the prisoners in my cell were all white. But there were all kinds of them, white-collar fraudsters in suits, transvestites, little streetwise thugs, armed robbers and drunks, all together, and then me in my denim jeans that had disintegrated from the salt because I liked to wade into the ocean on hot days at Sea Point and then walk along the shore in wet jeans in the baking sun. They were patched and had patches over the patches. Hardly any denim was visible. My hair was long and bleached white by sea and sun.

I was just a Cape Town hip cat who'd strayed too far, but I had the ability to look tough in the minds and fantasies of other people. Guys didn't mess with me because I fulfilled a certain stereotype. In my head I was this little *wuss*, living in a dream world, on one hand deeply cynical, but so fucking naive at the same time.

I was thinking of poetry and songs and who knows what else. I wasn't a criminal. I wasn't a proper drug dealer. I didn't have it in me to be one, because I was a useless businessman, inefficient at getting rid of the merchandise because I found no pleasure in negotiating with people.

There was a toilet in the cell, set very close to the corridor where the 'wall' was nothing but a giant metal grille like a zoo cage, with a similar grilled door on one side. There was a little privacy wall, about three feet high and four feet long, on the other side of the toilet, but it was ineffective in a jam-packed cell. I felt uneasy at first about using the toilet in the middle of a group of people. Nobody turned away discreetly when a man sat on the throne, and any noises received a smattering of applause, particularly loud farting craps, which got applause and cheers even from neighbouring cells. Smelly shits, on the other hand, always earned a chorus of boos and usually started a debate about 'What the fuck were you eating last night?'

And just what the fuck were we eating? I don't know where John Vorster Square got its food. Some know-it-all claimed that we were fed the leftovers from one of the hospitals in town. Breakfast was always a mug of cold coffee and a slice of brown bread and the two other meals were usually some kind of tasteless maize product that I had never eaten before, also accompanied by a slice of brown bread. It was always terrible fare and there was never enough to fill a man's belly. The nights were long and hungry for those who didn't have tobacco to fill the void.

It was a long weekend, so I had to wait until Tuesday morning before I appeared in court. But nobody messed with me and I made it

JOHN VORSTER SQUARE

through the time. Getting ready for court was a relief after days of lying and sitting and walking in depressed circles and shitting in public. We were marched out, numbered and sorted, handcuffed and put in a khaki prison truck, which drove us across town to the courthouse. I felt like a monkey in a cage, visible through the wire, just feet away from people stopping to cross a street, some looking up, girls too, all on their way to work with that fresh morning scrub, looking up and seeing us being trucked off to some terrible place and they just look. No one screams for help. There is no help. Just a truckload of bad luck.

I have never seen anything like what I saw under the courthouse. There were huge cells that could hold hundreds of people, and we were lined up, one after the other, in this vast underground labyrinth of incarceration, the awesome sense of space, which a year later would be full to the brim. They were planning ahead. All these cells were for the troublemakers. They were just waiting. Waiting.

Business was good. There were always a lot of people after a long weekend. Our cuffs were removed and we were marched single file into the cells. The sound of keys, always the swinging of keys, *kachung kachung kachung*, but above it, down from the main hall, comes the sound of singing, maybe five hundred men ... all singing their own twisted chorus to 'Dark Side of the Moon' ... as we round the corner ... Welcome ... to the dark side ...

Kachung kachung kachung.

... of the moon ... Welcome to the dark side of the moon.

On my own among hundreds of strangers all exhibiting tension and worry, all waiting for the show to begin, the next decree from above. This was not where I wanted to be. I wanted to be on a sunshiny university campus with pretty girls tossing their hair as we sat on the stairs of some architectural wonder, debating and laughing. Debating and laughing. And all the men sang.

Welcome to the dark side of the moon.

When the time for my appearance came, I was taken from the

dark side to a small cell situated as a feeder to a courtroom. It was like being backstage at a concert. We waited, about six of us in a little room, waiting for the bailiff to call our names. Backstage in the dressing room of crime, we prepared for our pirouette before justice.

There was a guy there hiring out his tie, so everybody went up, one after the other, wearing the same tie, like they'd all graduated from the same old school, the school of hard knocks. Written high up on the walls of the cell were the stories of the lost, the poems of heartbreak and betrayal, and little ditties to The Pimp, which is what they called a traitor, a turncoat, a rat. Their names were written there too. The lowest of the low, the traitors' list – memorise it, brother, in case you meet them. You snoozed and you lost. Loser!

I was called up the stairs and there I was, the antithesis of all that was happening there in those halls of justice, the system and the organisation, men with careers and pensions all working in this system that served apartheid and kept the Happy White People safe. Presiding over it all was the old judge who had his lifetime of achievement behind him, his youth on the farm and his time at university, and all those years as a lawyer in private practice, with his family and his grandchildren and his glorious career. And there in front of him was me, with my long hair sun-bleached and dirty after four days without a shower, my jeans tattered and embroidered. Perhaps he knew my grandfather.

Twenty years old and in front of the judge – this is one memory that he will never have. At twenty he was playing rugby for his university team and getting drunk with the boys on the weekend, and maybe shooting the odd black man as a rite of passage. At the request of the police, who had written 'no bail' in red across the top of my file, the judge ordered me to be held without bail, under something called Section 13, without any access to the outside world until my next appearance.

I had no idea what the fuck was going on. I hadn't cooperated. I hadn't given them names … or anything. I had told them, 'It's only me, I am guilty. There is no other name.' Maybe they thought, or had been led to believe, that I was some kind of big connection. What the fuck was going on?

Everyone was quiet in the truck on the way back to John Vorster Square, which, I learnt on subsequent court visits, was the way it always went. In the morning it was all full bellies, brushed hair and perhaps even the promise of release if all went well, but those who made the return trip were hungry, tired and depressed. And silent.

John Vorster Square was a police station where law breakers were brought in and charged, but there were sections where people were 'remanded' and stayed in a kind of long-term limbo. I had been remanded back to John Vorster for a few weeks till the next appearance date. Nobody told me anything else. I wasn't issued with that essential manual, *Now That You Are in Trouble: Helpful Hints for First-Time Criminals*.

At the time I had no concept of my rights. I could see the world in terms of 'fair and unfair' or 'nice and not nice' or even 'right and wrong', but when bad things were done to me I just accepted it as what happened in the world, trying to roll with the punches and land on my feet. From the beginning I knew that I had lost and 'they' had won, and I made no demands whatsoever on 'the system'. I just assumed that lawyers were for rich people and if you weren't rich you just rotted. I knew that money bought you the things you needed, and I had no money. If I'd had money and lawyers in the first place I would never have been in prison. It never occurred to me to demand my rights. It was South Africa. I simply assumed that I had no inherent rights on planet earth.

After the prison truck returned to John Vorster Square I was handed over to a policeman who escorted me back upstairs.

'So, how'd it go in court today?' he asked me, making light conversation.

'Well, I'm back here so …' I shrugged my shoulders.

'So no bail then?'

'No, no bail at all.' I told him what the judge said about Section 13, but that I didn't know what it meant.

What it meant, he explained, shaking his head in commiseration, was *baie kak* for me. Under Section 13 I could have no visitors, no phone calls, no newspapers and no lawyers until special investigations had been completed.

Fuck!

Back in the cell, I slept on the cold concrete floor and dreamt of tobacco.

CARL

I met Carl in that cell. I'd seen him in an office being questioned on my first day, when I was being charged and printed and so on. There were so many things going on, but I remember seeing him and his father sitting at a desk and conversing with the Colonel. At one point I'd heard Carl's father shouting, 'Lock him up! Lock him up for ten years! I want nothing more to do with him.'

But Carl was treated differently from me, and he wasn't subjected to the rough handling and mockery by all and sundry. It was the first time that I had met an Afrikaner Prince.

Carl and I got along. We had a different headspace than most of the people there. We looked different. We were young and beautiful compared to the others, many of whom exhibited physical symptoms of the shitty life that kept them coming back to places like this.

Carl told me later that the same people who set me up set him up, that our fates were connected. I doubted that, but then I really had no idea what had happened, whether it was just an accident, a by-product of stupidity, or an actual soul-slave deal, done with a decision, executed with precision, by somebody.

Somehow Carl and I got transferred out of the regular cells with the riff-raff and we were put on the other side of the building. I try to remember why. Were the cells overcrowded, or did Carl hypnotise the guards with his elegant upper-class Afrikaner charm? Maybe it was because we were being remanded for a few weeks instead of being sent to the real remand centre at The Fort, a proper prison in uptown Joburg.

If you walked from that cattle pen area with about eight or ten cells, each packed to the brim, and turned right down another corridor, you came to the black men's holding area. Apartheid. So close. Black and white criminals separated by a wall and a right turn at the end of the passage. But if you went the other way, past the guard station and the elevator and down another long, lonely corridor and through two metal gates, there was a little private wing of about four cells. These cells actually had windows and you could see the sky. Unfortunately they also had wind, as the windows had no glass and it was the middle of winter.

That's where they took us. Carl, with his mysterious hypnotic power, the piercing blue eyes, arranged for the cops to move us. How the hell did he do that? Was he an undercover cop? It certainly makes you wonder, but there was a lot of strangeness going down. He said he was into L. Ron Hubbard and Scientology. He said his dad, apparently a well-known citizen, had deserted him in this time of trouble, and that his grandmother had just died and left him some money which his mother was funnelling to help him with a lawyer.

Carl had a persuasive manner, but who was he conning? Me or them? Was he really connected to the same affair as me? I wasn't connected to anyone except for Poison Pete, who had helped by raising seed money back home. I was a solo act. Carl and I spent maybe six weeks together there in that cell. I found that holding me under Section 13 for 'further investigation and enquiries' mostly meant hitting me in a chair and generally having some fun. Was it really six weeks?

I could see no way out. I was really and truly fucked. All around me were walls and men with keys and weapons. I was going to see five or ten years thrown at me by some motherless pig dog. I had no one to give me hope. I had no money, no lawyer, nothing with which to bribe the judge and grease the system. Locked up and powerless, claustrophobic, just me and Carl sitting in a concrete room. Dreaming of tobacco.

There was no bed in the cell. There was only a toilet, without a wall or any privacy, controlled by a silver button set in the wall. *Flush*, it said. We were isolated there. In the morning they brought cold watery coffee in a milk bottle and a couple of slices of cheap brown bread smeared with white margarine.

We cleaned the toilet. We scrubbed it and washed it. They didn't give us water to drink, so it was our waterhole. We had to use it for water. We drank the toilet water of John Vorster Square. Would an undercover cop do that? Perhaps if he had all the right medical care he might. We washed in it, drank from it ... and used it as a toilet. Once a week we were allowed to shower in cold water and use the communal razors to shave with soap. Blood, the stinky shared blood of the hep cats.

I didn't pray or call on any of the usual spirits that my family had worshipped for the past eighteen hundred years, that good old boy, Yahweh, Jehovah, God and his Prophets of Profit. I wasn't in the kneeling mood. I had done the Sunday school thing and it all seemed interesting but silly, but still I felt the need to believe. Are human beings hard-wired that way? So I believed in water. The elemental.

I crouched in front of the toilet, on my knees with soap to clean the bowl, but on my knees nevertheless, and I would whisper messages to the water. It was our only connection to the outside world. I imagined that water flowing out to the ocean, even though we were eight hundred kilometres from the nearest beach. I would whisper little missives and endearments that would flow deep under the city past the mineshafts and the gold, into rivers and on into the sea, the first mother of creation, where we all came from, dreaming perhaps from some ancient genetic memory, dreaming of the first times when we moved like poetry in the darkness of life, long before we crawled up onto the land with our big brains and our little schemes.

Religion. What you believe in. What you give your money to. What inspires you. What lifts up your spirit and makes you quake in your boots. What comforts you when you are cold and alone.

The windows were about six feet high by three feet wide, and the cold air sometimes howled through the bars. They were set a few inches higher than the top of my head, and there was no window sill to stand on, because it was cut at a forty-five-degree angle, but if you jumped up hard and slammed your fingertips against the metal mesh, there was a good chance a couple of fingers would find purchase, slipping through the small holes just enough to pull closer and rearrange both hands, and then like some kind of insect pressed up against the window, splayed sideways, you could see the street below, with cars and normal people.

We were in the isolation wing, but we weren't alone. In the cell next to us was an Orthodox Jewish guy who sang old prayer laments at very unorthodox hours, and had all these kosher sausages hanging from the bars of his cell door as there was no furniture inside. His crime was that he was the brother of a man who had had some mental episode and had taken a rifle and started shooting people dead from a window in the Israeli embassy in Pretoria.

The logic of a police state is that you lock the shooter up deep underground somewhere and do who knows what to him, but you also arrest and incarcerate his poor brother, *just in case*. He had already been there in limbo for half a year. In a democracy you don't put a man in jail for the crime his brother committed, but in a police state you can let your dreams go wild, baby. But police state or not, this sad and confused young man had a lawyer and the lawyer demanded that his client be treated properly as a Jew. The police state, busy at the time doing huge arms deals with Israel, honoured these religious demands by allowing him a full kosher diet and regular visits from his rabbi. Whenever we were taken for a shower and shave, Carl and I grabbed some of his hanging food. Times were tough. We were always hungry.

In the cell next to him was a Portuguese guy. Every now and then the men from BOSS came padding past us to see him and then he wailed and cried.

'I-a-know-a-nutting, I-a-know-a-nutting. Pliz, pliz, pliz...'

It was 1975. Did they have little hidden cameras back then or tiny microphones discreetly built into the walls or the light fixtures? I don't know what kind of tech was available then. Was Carl a cop? Was this some kind of info-gathering session, a proving ground, a training mission, a deep-cover penetration? The whole thing was surreal and bizarre.

16

A GUY CAN GO FAR IN FIFTY SECONDS

The first week they came every day to take me to the talking room. Big investigations. They wanted me to tell them something, some things, information about my organisation and silly stuff like that. Someone led them to believe that I was Somebody and they thought I was just acting stupid. So they kept asking me questions.

They wanted to know about Donny. Who was with me in the Volksie, they asked. What was his name? Where was he hiding? Where did he live? They called him 'my partner'. I lied to them, but I told them the truth too, and I focused on the truth to make my lies real. He was not my partner (the truth), he was just a guy I'd met along the road, another hippy drifter, and I simply gave him some money to drive me (not so true).

'True as god!' I said. 'Jesus, fuck, I never saw the guy before in my life. I swear it, I swear, I wouldn't lie. I don't know his last name, all I know is his name is Deon, and he comes from Port Elizabeth. Believe me, I would tell you if I knew, he's no friend of mine, but I don't know. We just rode and listened to music and smoked cigarettes. I didn't ask him his life story. True as fucking god.'

It was always the same cop who came to get me, the *gofer*, the fetcher, the one they called the Jew, with his nine-millimetre Parabellum. The first day he took me for *some talking* he had a different gun; he had a Magnum Small Penis, big fucker of a gun, and I walked with him out of John Vorster Square, through the glass doors. He stopped at the top of the stairs.

'How about I give you fifteen seconds?' he said with a toss of the head, sweeping some imaginary forelock from his eyes.

'What?'

'Fifteen seconds. You run. I give you fifteen seconds, then I come after you. Fair and square.'

Who wrote this guy's script? Still, it was tempting and he knew it. Freedom. The chance to run. The next day he upped his offer.

'Okay, I'll give you twenty seconds.'

I was raised in full post-war propaganda. English war films, Battler Britton and Sergeant Rock. Germans were bad and Englishmen and Jews were good. Yanks were okay too in their tacky way. The whole Second World War paradigm. *They died to save the world from tyranny. Savage racism at its worst!* In apartheid society in Cape Town, people still worshipped these ideals, and it seemed so strange (to me) because all around us was a racist police state. Everything but the death camps.

The very first Jewish school in South Africa evolved into what is now Cape Town High School, situated at the top of the Gardens across from the Mount Nelson Hotel, and where I spent five years from 1967 to 1971. Behind the main school building there was an old library and art room which was once the Jewish schoolhouse. In my day, many of the established Jewish families still sent their kids there, and my class was always about one-third Jewish, one-third English and one-third Euro-mongrel, and so, by social osmosis, I felt partly Jewish, partly English and somewhat of a *brak*.

In 1967, my first year in high school, some classmates' older cousins and brothers went off to serve in the Israeli military during the Six-Day War against Egypt. As a thirteen-year-old I had not yet learnt to question the stories we read as 'accurate history', so it seemed right that the good guys, Israel, 'us', would beat the evil Mighty Egypt that had enslaved them and made their lives so miserable all those years ago in biblical times.

On the weekends I went to Sunday school and studied Hebrew legends about Abraham, Jacob, Samson, King David and Daniel in the lion's den. I was familiar with the name Nebuchadnezzar and the trouble-making fire-walking trio Shadrach, Meshach and Abednego. In fact, at age thirteen, I knew more about mythical Israeli families than I ever knew about my own family trees.

Every Sunday the church bells rang. Every morning when I woke up I heard the imams calling faithful Muslims to prayer from the mosques in the city. Cape Town is a Muslim city in many ways. When the Dutch first colonised the area, their Christian theology said it was wrong to enslave Christians, so when they brought slaves to the Cape they did not convert them. Instead they were encouraged to associate with, and become, Muslims. It was 'kosher' for the good Christian Dutch burghers to keep Muslim slaves. No problems there, dude.

The first music show I ever played was for a boy's bar mitzvah party. All around Cape Town were followers of the Middle Eastern god, Jehovah, Allah, Elohim, he whose name must not be spoken, introduced to the world by Abraham from Iraq (Ur). There was still some questionable Jew-joke 'humour' that was 'acceptable', but nobody talked like those cops talked to the Jew. Not in Cape Town anyway. On the fifth day the Jew offered me fifty seconds. As we walked down the wide stairs he stopped as usual and pointed at the street.

'Fifty seconds, man. A guy can go far in fifty seconds. Look – you could be around that corner before I even started.'

It was all so casual. The man was a fool. If I was a real psycho I would have jumped him and broken his neck and made off with his Penis Protector.

'Why do you let them talk to you that way?' I asked him.

'You don't know anything,' he sneered at me.

'I know what it sounds like,' I intoned in a know-it-all manner.

'You have no idea. You are the one in trouble and I'm trying to help you, so fuck you. You get no more chances. Go now. Fucking mooove it!'

We walked across to the big office tower. The Talking House. I could feel this guy near some kind of breaking point, and maybe questioning him was a stupid thing to have done. Maybe he would just shoot me in the street and say I made a break. True to his word, he never offered me running time again and refused to talk to me after that. He shut me out. I'd failed him somehow.

Some weird safety door opened in my mind and the part of the brain reserved for crises took over. It was as if some emergency override programme that had sat dormant until then sprang to life and, strangely enough, I found that I had a perverse sense of gallows humour, a liberating giddy feeling like laughing while trying to drink champagne at a wedding, and the bubbles and giggles become mixed, one going down and one going up, so when I saw that I was here and they were there and they kept telling me, *All you have to do is play along, just get with the system and there are all kinds of benefits waiting*, I just couldn't hold it back.

Why, if I played my cards right they might just set me free and provide me with a ticket out of the country if that's what I really wanted. *Just get with the programme, boy. The programme got you here and now you have to join in and give us a little something.* It was hilarious.

The basic premise until then was that I was the stupid drug dealer who had sold the 680 Durban Poison sticks to resourceful undercover policemen who had arrested me and written up a statement which I had signed as true. The next task for the policemen was to find my secrets and take down more stupid criminals. Until then I had just gone along with that narrative (albeit stubbornly), but on this particular day I had the cop's phrase bouncing about in my skull, 'A man can go far in fifty seconds', and I found it hilariously poetic. I wondered if he had made it up himself or taken it from a Hollywood film. It sounded like a Clint Eastwood cliché.

I decided to be creative and change the story and went with the first thing that came out of my mouth.

'The stuff was all mine,' I stated, 'for personal use, to smoke.'

'What?' demanded Boetman. 'You sold that dagga to us.'

'No I didn't. I don't remember doing that, it was all just personal. I am changing my statement.' I knew that the money from the transaction was gone and the only evidence left was the dagga.

There was some hitting involved, but I don't think they really liked hitting me. I didn't fight back. There wasn't any point. Not in a room full of laughing people with guns and black boots.

After some hours or some days, maybe it was weeks, I decided on a plan. I'd originally said that I got the stuff from 'some guy I met by the beach'. I came back with a new twist and acted like I was coming round to their point of view.

'I wasn't quite telling the truth, Boetman,' I finally admitted. 'There's a place where I got the stuff. It's in the country, though, out in the bundu, but I can take you there.'

I thought maybe if we could go out on a road trip I would find a way to jump ship, make a break. They hemmed and hawed about it a bit, demanding the location, the name of a person, some concrete details.

'It's complicated, out in the country. I'm not from there so I don't know all the names, just how to get there.'

I could see the smugness. He thought I was finished opposing him. I was just a weak little person with no more petrol in my two-stroke rebel tank.

'How do you know this place?'

Does he believe me? How can I tell what he is scheming? This cat, for sure, is no jive-talkin' idiot, but the way he's sitting back, is he acting?

'From the guy I met at the beach. I've been there lots of times.' I acted nervous. I was nervous.

'Ja, well, it's a fucken 500-mile trip.'

A day or two later we were back in the room and he changed his tune. 'So maybe we can,' he smirked, 'go on *holiday* to Durban with you, but you have to give us more information.'

I wasn't feeling so good that day about the feasibility of outrunning a Parabellum with dum-dum bullets. Also, that funny bone kicked in, you know, the Merry Prankster of Death? The hysterical Joke of Eternity when you know you are well and truly fucked. That day I was the laughing Buddha.

'I changed my mind. I can't take you.' I hadn't thought about it. It just popped out of my mouth. I was rocking with a deep silent laughter. These guys were elevating me to a higher plane of consciousness, or else I was really losing it.

'Don't you mess with us!' He pointed his finger at me, just in case I thought he was talking about someone else.

'Your shoes.' I pointed at his oversized chunky black lace-ups with the thick leather soles and shook my head sadly from side to side. 'If you wear shoes like that, they'll spot you as a cop right away and shoot us all dead.'

'Shoot?'

I nodded vigorously. 'Yes – please don't wear those shoes,' I pleaded.

'Who sells them the guns? Do you sell them the guns?' The Detective Sergeant was losing it. He must have just worked out the Durban trip with a superior officer. 'Don't fuck with me, *takhaar*. I been on a thousand undercover raids and I don't need no *fokken* shoes.'

'Then I can't do it, no, no, no. You have to be in disguise. They'll kill us all.'

I was sitting on a chair at the side of Boetman's desk and, as his patience evaporated and his frustration grew, he reached out and grabbed a fistful of my long hair in his large hand, pulling me off the chair and down towards his right shoe, which rose fast and hard, smashing into my mouth. I still have the scar there. It turned into a festering sore that wouldn't heal. I think I laughed or maybe I cried. Sometimes they are so close, those two, you don't even need a visa to cross over.

I am the laughing Buddha.

'Come on, guys, let's get some coffee.' The big man got up and headed for the door, leaving me on the floor. It was shiny, smooth and cool on the skin, different from the concrete in the cell. The rest of the detectives followed Boetman, leaving one cat behind, a fatherly demeanour about him with his silverside hair, and he came over and helped me up.

'Ag, man, you got to play it smarter with those guys,' he said in his homey small-town Afrikaans accent. 'Here, want a smoke?' He offered an open pack of Van Rijn Filters in the fliptop yellow box.

'Thanks,' I said as he lit it for me.

'Want a drink?' he asked as he walked over to one of the desks.

'What?' I looked at him suspiciously.

'A drink, a *dop*, some brandy?' He pulled a glass from a drawer and poured a generous half-glass of Commando brandy. 'You know, if you work it out with those guys, things can get much easier for you.' He opened another drawer and pulled out slabs of yellow Moroccan hashish, tossing them on the table next to my drink. 'You can have anything you like.'

'I just want to leave this place behind.' I confessed my religion.

'Why? It's not so bad here.' He really was convincing. I already liked him and his caring words, the good sense he made, but I still acted the churl for his benefit. In real life, with sane people and normal cognitive patterns, this part of the interrogation was the part where I was supposed to keep my mouth shut. Zip it. Don't say anything, *skaapie*!

But. The problem is, I grew up in Cape Town and I was horribly infected with a severe recurring case of Long Street Foul Mouth Syndrome and I just couldn't stop.

'Why?' I muttered. 'Why! Because the prime minister is a *poes*.'

Nice Guy flinched and his mouth hardened around the edges and suddenly he started looking more like those BOSS agents.

'No,' I corrected myself, 'Vorster is a *fokken poeslap!*'

'You know,' he said, taking a step back, straightening his back and squaring his shoulder, 'that is slander, *crimen injuria*, and you can earn yourself an additional three years for that. Don't be stupid. You are still a young, good-looking guy. Whatever happens, you must think of your life and your family and get this business out of the way. What are your plans for the future?'

(Shut up, shut up, shut up, shut up.)

'Well fuck that *verlep ou poesface!*' (Please don't say any more. Look at the cop. Read the room, and you will see that he is hoping for something a little more contrite.) '*E'sê vir hom ... sy ma se fok se moer ... jou tief-naai jentoe!*'

The cop's mouth opened as if to speak, but I had the floor and there was no stopping me.

'So ... you and that *poeskas* prime minister can lock me up for as long as you like ...' (I think this is where my guardian angel just gave up and cowered under a desk with her eyes firmly shut) '... and when I get out of jail I'm going to leave this stinking shithole country, *hierdie kakland*, behind and I'm going to Russia where I'll train to be a Big Communist General and then we will come back, me and the whole Russian Army, and when the war is over we will put a Kaffir King in every fucking Transvaal town. That ... is my plan.'

I sat back, quite pleased with my answer, and raised my brandy to my lips as Mister Nice Guy looked at me aghast, but I never got to drink it, because The Guys had come back, quietly, and the Big Black Shoe booted me out of the chair, my glass smashing against the wall, brandy streaming over papers.

'Saddle up, boys, we have another fool to catch. And you,' Boetman said to the Jew, 'take this stupid *kafferboetie* back to his cell, and get a fucken *boy* to clean up this mess.'

After a few weeks of this kind of fun I was told by a guard one evening to be ready to go to court bright and early the next day. The one big downside to being isolated in that cell was that they often forgot to bring us breakfast. You never knew when it would arrive, and when it did it was the usual cold coffee and bread.

That morning I waited hopefully for my breakfast because, crappy as it was, it was at least something, but I was taken away to court long before the food came and I told Carl, over my shoulder, to enjoy his double helping. At least I had some cigarettes to dull the hunger pangs. I had been locked up for only a few weeks but, compounded with the stress of the whole situation, it really did seem much longer than that, and having a change from the daily routine of boredom and fear was invigorating. I had tried my best to look presentable but with questionable success. My hair was uncombed and greasy and I wore the big baggy purple jersey to keep me warm. The clothes I was wearing were the ones I was arrested in, the same ones I wore all day and often slept in on very cold nights. Once again I climbed into the prisoner truck and sat with all the losers looking at real life through the wire mesh.

Even though it was terrible to be trucked around on display in a cage, visible to everybody, that brief journey to the courthouse was the best part of the day. I got to see the one thing that had disappeared from my world. Girls and women. They all looked so beautiful with their hair and make-up perfect, all briskly on their way to work. Nothing could compare with real live girls in motion. Some of the guys weren't content with merely looking at the girls and began whistling and cat-calling, which didn't seem to impress any of them, and some turned up their noses and tossed their heads, visibly disturbed by the violation of their airspace by low-life criminals in a truck. Not exactly the best way to impress a girl.

At the courthouse we were offloaded and led single file to where the officials with clipboards called out the accused prisoners by name and marched them off to their respective waiting rooms. I was taken straight to the same basement holding cell under the court, bypassing the massive cells where all the men had been singing their welcome to the dark side of the moon on my first visit. There were only three of us waiting, fidgeting and worrying, me in my scruffy attire feeling more down at heel than ever next to the other two fellows in their cheap, badly fitting jackets and mismatched ties. One by one the other guys were called up, returning with rather crestfallen looks on their faces, and finally the voice yelled from above.

'Rautenbach!'

To describe this court appearance as premature ejaculation would be overstating the length of the affair. I couldn't tell whether the judge was the same one as before, but the prosecutor jumped up immediately, stating my name, and requested that I be remanded back to John Vorster Square. The judge agreed, banging his little wooden hammer on the desk. That was it. I had no idea what to do, it was all so one-sided. The judge didn't speak to me and nobody got up claiming to be representing me, so I just went back down the stairs as instructed by the uniformed official. Was I supposed to shout at the judge? Ask him for bail? I had no money, so asking for bail didn't seem an option. I just got shunted ignorantly down the railroad of justice. They had trucks waiting to take us back when the courts adjourned for lunch (without offering us any) and the ride back wasn't as inspiring as the morning trip. The traffic was thick and toxic fumes belched from trucks and cars as I went over and over in my head what I should have done and should have said, but it was too late. I got back to John Vorster Square just in time to find that I had missed lunch there too.

I needed to make a plan.

One Flew Over the Cuckoo's Nest hadn't been made into a film yet, but I had read the Ken Kesey book and been quite taken with it, except that our anti-hero ends up getting done in with a frontal lobotomy to stifle his obnoxious humanity and is finally smothered to death with a pillow to restore his dignity. Then the friend who killed him with the pillow has a big awakening and smashes a hole in a wall of the mental hospital and runs off into the dawn. I was thinking about running into that dawn. I was remembering all the times that I woke up at the side of a country road, under the trees in my sleeping bag, the sky just growing light, and I would start walking, feeling loose and free, walking into the dawn with that fresh morning scent. Just me and the gravel at the side of the road.

I started thinking about mental hospitals – about how easy it was for me to scoot off on my wheelchair from F3 at Groote Schuur, and how easy it always seemed to be for Harry to run away from Valkenberg. I wanted to avoid ten years in prison, so I started thinking seriously about finding some way to put in a plea of insanity – not psycho-killer insanity, more 'mental incompetence due to a break with reality' kind of crazy – so that I could get to an easier place to think and to make a plan for freedom. With no control in the halls of justice, I knew that I would be sentenced at the whim of authorities and be stuck behind heavily guarded stone walls, but if I could just see my way into a mental hospital, which is a pretty mental idea in the first place, then who knows what could happen?

Ever since I heard that my Boer grandfather had shot a nun in the leg and spent almost a decade in Valkenberg, and even though I never got to know old Oupa Piet, I needed to be crazy. I wanted to be crazy: it would explain everything.

In the meantime I just had to pass the time.

I still had most of my forty rand, plus Carl got some money smuggled in, and we started buying booze from one of the guards, who themselves were drinking on the job pretty hard at night, and we would get totally pissed on Bols brandy in John Vorster Square. I may not have folded and talked in interrogation, but sitting through the late winter night drinking brandy and Cokes and smoking Texan cigarettes, I probably talked a lot and so, if Carl was an undercover agent, he knew every single thing about big-mouth me. And if the place was wired, bugged, then they knew what and who I was.

Two people in a concrete room twenty-four hours a day. You become acquainted.

Carl's mother kept coming by, slipping him large chunks of change from the inheritance his grandmother had left him. Somehow this woman managed to get a huge cardboard box of supplies sent to our cell, a trove of treasures which included a decent-sized transistor radio with spare batteries, some smokes and a pack of about eight boxes of matches. Technically, according to the standard rules of confinement, we were not supposed to have matches. They were always in short supply, and we usually used a razor blade, which we were also not supposed to have, and sliced each Lion-brand wooden match into four quarters to make them last.

There were dozens of books in the box and I finally got to read the entire Kurt Vonnegut collection, *The Gulag Archipelago* by Aleksandr Solzhenitsyn and all four books of Lawrence Durrell's *Alexandria Quartet. Justine. Balthazar. Mountolive. Clea.* There were two yoga books and I perfected the technique of standing on my head like a yogi. There was also a little camping stove, with instant coffee and sugar. It was ridiculous, but there we were, smoking cigarettes and drinking Nescafé made with toilet water. Carl got really tight with one of the cops, a sad sensitive cat with financial problems, and lent him four hundred rand to get him out of debt. Blind eyes were turning left and right.

I also read *Papillon*, the story of a man's escape from the French penal colony Devil's Island.

Sometimes when the BOSS agents came, with their silver suits and deadpan CIA expressions, to interrogate the Portuguese guy two cells down, they would have a young black guy in a suit tagging along. Someone said that he was studying to be a lawyer but worked in the prison. As he walked behind them he would make funny faces like the class clown, and every time he passed our cell he would throw a little stick of ganja through the bars, walking on and never looking back.

I have no idea why he did that, but anything to help the stone-cold minutes tick themselves away. I couldn't figure out if it was a trap, another ploy by the cops, but nothing ever came of it. We would sit there all day reading, smoking cigarettes and drinking instant coffee, and at night, while the fluorescent tubes hummed (they never turned the lights off in John Vorster Square), we would smoke weed rolled in newspaper, drink brandy and listen to the radio.

Around two or three in the morning we would be as drunk as a guy could get, with that acrid taste of brandy and Coke in the nose, and we'd crank the music to the max, listening to LM Radio playing the hits of the day: John Lennon's 'Whatever Gets You Through the Night' and Sweet with 'Fox on the Run', the two of us line-dancing glam-rock drunkards with a Motown marching groove, screaming at the top of our voices.

But there was nothing more poignantly appropriate than sitting there, thick-brained on brandy in a concrete prison room in the ice cold of winter at three in the morning and hearing The Band doing 'I Shall Be Released'.

I see my light come shining...

Then, just as we were winding The Party down, getting ready for sleep, the feverishly religious young man in the next cell would start reciting the Talmud and sing Holy Israel songs. We made our noise in shifts.

The big problem was trying to figure out how to get rid of the brandy bottle the next day when the day shift came on. It was like a game. You are in a room with no furniture and some empty bottles to dispose of ... I think we tried breaking them very small and putting the pieces down the toilet but that wasn't very successful.

Eventually Carl bribed or persuaded one of the guards to go down to the women's section and hunt us up a couple of foam mattresses so we didn't have to lie on the cold concrete any more. How did he do that? The mattress I got was very thick so I broke a brandy bottle and sliced deep into the foam. Every night I would put another bottle in there and smash the shit out of it.

After a month I was sleeping on a mattress filled with glass.

★★★★★★★★★★ **17** ★★★★★★★★★★

ZIP NOLAN

For a few weeks it was quite crazy, with the boere coming late at night to have their sport with me. Sometimes they would come so late that me and Carl would be totally pissed on brandy and Carl would try to karate-kick the cops as they took me down the cold passageway.

'Come on!' he would scream. 'Come! One at a time, I'll take you on!'

They never took him on. They never questioned him. Always me.

The cops were usually wasted on Commando brandy by this time of night, so they didn't even notice our level of inebriation. All the guards in charge of prisoners were pretty sizzled too. It was just one big drinking party with handcuffs and guns, like a gay sadomasochistic fantasy. It would have been more fun if they had Nazi bitches in leather skirts with blouses inevitably too small (wartime rationing, probably) and ripped mesh stockings like in those True War pulp books.

At this stage, Boetman and his cronies must have still believed that I was a kingpin connection of some sort, because they invested many hours taking me all the way down to the ground floor and across to the Talking Building for their late-night interrogation sessions. Quite possibly they simply found me entertaining, because I didn't respond in the 'normal' way, begging for forgiveness or trying to make a bargain.

What they were doing was also totally illegal, even according to the pseudo laws of the country. There were protocols to be followed and there was paperwork to be filed, even for taking a prisoner for questioning, especially at night, because most of the routine work was a daylight affair. But Boetman himself would come swaggering in like he was on a jol, flanked always by a couple of henchmen, and he'd simply order the uniformed policeman on duty to hand me over.

Strangely, although there was a lot of verbal threatening about what they would do if I didn't cooperate, I was never strapped to a wall and whipped or electrocuted or even burned with cigarettes. Mostly it was playground bully stuff, shoving my face into the wall as we walked or tripping me and watching me roll down the stairs with my hands cuffed behind my back, which is not as easy as it looks. One time they tried to give me a treatment they called The Windmill, a procedure in which the prisoner's hands and feet were cuffed together and a broomstick inserted behind the knees. The broomstick/prisoner combo was then lifted up off the floor and placed between two desks, which supported each end of the contraption. Then the poor victim was spun round and round and round. At least that was what was supposed to happen, but on this occasion the damn stick broke before they could manoeuvre me into position and I hit my head hard on the floor.

I suspect there were legal constraints holding them back from beating me to a pulp (unlike their security brethren, who could do anything imaginable), so most of the violence was Hollywoodesque, all punches to the stomach and slapping the face and head to highlight their dialogue.

'What is your partner's name?' (Slap.)

'Where is your partner hiding?' (Slap.)

'Where does he live?' (Slap.)

'Who do you work for?' (Slap.)

A barrage of these boring questions was often underscored by kicking the chair over, which wasn't that bad in the daytime sessions, because I was never handcuffed and could protect my head as I fell, but at night they always kept the cuffs on, sometimes fastening me to the chair itself, which made the experience a little more dangerous. Still, they never really seemed serious about hurting.

I think Boetman loved his job. At the time there was no revolution in the streets and the drug boys were the rock stars of the SAP and seemed to be having the time of their lives. The drug squad could get away with all sorts of shit. They could wear cool outfits, drink, take drugs in the name of undercover operations and shoot anybody that ran away. In America President Nixon's war on drugs was at a peak, and the Hollywood narrative of the time reflected this with films like *The French Connection*, *Serpico*, the *Death Wish* series and the *Dirty Harry* franchise. These cops seemed to think they were movie stars too, because they all appeared to have modelled their walk and talk on those fictional characters.

The uniformed policemen who served as guards were a completely different bunch, polar opposites to the slick drug squad hipsters, and most of them looked more depressed than me. Carl and I wondered if this was the end of the career line, a dumping ground for useless cops.

One of the guards was a legend, very undisciplined apparently, but also one of the most decorated for his time on the South West African border, fighting SWAPO and perhaps doing some Angola-bashing. A war hero. Rumour was that he would've been tossed out of the police force, because they said he just didn't give a fuck, if not for his legendary battle record, so he was posted to the cells guarding criminals and losers with the fatties and drunks, the dead-end cops who all ended up here. He must have done some super shit at some or other time, because he was always treated with deference and respect by the other cops.

He wore blue aviator sunglasses, just like the comic character Zip Nolan, the American Highway State Patrol Officer with his sunglasses and helmet. Our Zip Nolan always had his shades on, even when he worked the night shift, and we used to make jokes about him. He just did his job as life went by. Mister Cool.

THE UNEXPLODED BOER

Then one night, one strange night, when the interrogators, Boetman and his henchmen, were dragging me down the passageway, still convinced by my idiotic attitude or by some informer that I had some information about something … old Zip Nolan stepped out of the guard room, the ugly fluorescent lights making his shades impenetrable, and he got between the bull-chested Boetman and me and he shook his head.

'Not tonight,' he said softly.

The cops stopped. They stopped pushing, pulling and dragging me.

'What?' Boetman's eyes widened momentarily in surprise and then narrowed to a single beam of malevolence. I could have sworn that he was going to punch old Zip in the face.

'If you want him, you have to go through me.'

Simple and clichéd, direct and to the point. Dirty Harry would have pissed in his pants.

'Enough.' He shook his head slowly, like he was already bored with the idea of talking to those armed *brekers*. He must have had some sort of kick-ass reputation, because old Boetman had quite a rep of his own for shooting first and asking questions later, but after about twenty seconds of cowboy stare, *mano a mano,* in the hard concrete midnight sun of John Vorster Square, Boetman and his sidekicks turned around and never came back.

Not that night. Not ever again. That was it. The whole thing just stopped. No more talking, no more punching, kicking, threatening, jeering, mocking and blackmailing. Maybe they had something going on, those two cops, some old bad blood perhaps, or maybe I was just such a pathetic sight trying to stay afloat in the deep end while the bullies threw rocks at me. Zip Nolan to the rescue again.

You find them in the most unusual places. Men of honour lost to this world.

THE PUSSY POSSE COMES TO TOWN

The utter powerlessness of incarceration. You just fall away. Through the window you can see the sky, one little corner of the road, or nothing. All day nothing with nobodies playing out the eternal game of predator and victim. You must just sit. Sit vas!

So lonely. It can be so lonely there behind the walls with strangers. I imagine heaven might be like that. It's all gone, all blown away, all thrown away. Outside people are making dinner, buying beer or just walking. Walking free in the street.

For the first week, my only visitor was Derek the Taxi Driver, who I was friends with from his time in Cape Town and Hout Bay. Donny and me, we had been staying at his flat before I got arrested, and he looked after my passport and my white leather suitcase and my belongings. I wasn't allowed to have visitors in the regular visiting rooms, but Derek rocked up with food and cigarettes and they let him come up to my cell to hand them over to me personally. He came twice, bringing magnificent bags of samoosas from Fietas.

This direct contact was a breakdown in the otherwise airtight isolation of Section 13 and, even though there was a watchful guard, he was just a bored policeman and not an obsessive secret agent, so Derek was able to relay messages from me to Donny, who was hiding out and afraid to go home to his family because he expected me to give his name to the police, but I was being stubborn. My message was always the same: 'Don't worry. I haven't given them your name. This is my problem and mine alone.' I had to get one thing right in that fucked-up Afterlife.

Then, out of the blue one day in the second week came my aunt, my mother's sister on the English side of my family. The bush telegraph had been working overtime and news of my arrest had quickly reached Cape Town and all the way to my mother. She didn't have the money for a lawyer, but she was clearly pulling out all the stops for me, because I had never met Aunt Lynette before. We were that kind of family. But here she was. *In times of trouble, rub this lantern, my young friend, and help shall surely appear in a cloud of smoke.*

They brought her upstairs, this aunt of mine, all the way to the fourth floor, through the entrance area, past the clamour of the regular population, and down the dim corridor all the way to my cell, where she was allowed briefly to talk to me through the bars of the door. Just like in the Western movies.

'Hello, Erich, I am your Aunt Lynette,' said the fierce-looking woman with the same jaw as me, inherited from some distant Viking relative. I knew that in her head she was judging me as a criminal druggie, but she held her tongue in check.

You may think that this is the most terrible way to meet a family member for the first time. Maybe so, but it was also the very best way. So what if we missed the birthdays, the Christmases, the Sunday dinners and the summer holidays? We were total strangers except for the fact that she was my mother's sister, and there in the belly of the beast, where most others turned their backs and ran away, fearful of contamination, she turned up with cigarettes and a few kind words.

My mother has told me since that Aunt Lynette 'knew some people' (South Africans often talked 'sotto voce' in that veiled British code) during and after the Rivonia Trial, at which Nelson Mandela was sentenced to life in the early sixties. Apparently she and her husband had 'helped some people' leave the country. For me she arrived bearing two cartons of Texan Filter cigarettes with the *rich, burly roast flavour*. She definitely understood the needs of inmates. Having my own cigarettes gave me some small control over the inescapable environment. And they were viable currency.

'Are you all right?' she asked.

I shrugged my shoulders and spread my hands. What could I say?

'Yes, I'm okay, I'll be okay. Thank you very much for the cigarettes, Auntie Lynn.'

She looked over her shoulder at the waiting policeman tapping his foot. 'I have to leave now,' she apologised. 'They said I must just give you the cigarettes and leave. She put her hand through the bars and squeezed my shoulder. 'Keep your chin up.'

The human touch is amazing. I put my hand on my shoulder where she had touched me as I watched her march away, policeman in tow, with her back straight and her head high, my mother's sister.

I was learning very quickly that visitors were the only real treasure that a prisoner could look forward to, but when you are in an alien town there isn't much chance of that. It seemed that the few acquaintances I had in Johannesburg had made a pact to deny my existence and there was nothing I could do about it.

My mother would have visited me regularly if I had been in Cape Town, but she still had two children at school, her job at the library and the little house in Sanddrift to pay for. But she did phone me and I was allowed to take the call, a sign that my Section 13 status had been rescinded. (Why did nobody ever tell me these things?) She told me that she had received a call from Carl's mother, who recommended that she phone the chief prosecutor to find out what was what. I told her my plan, the only defence I could concoct, hoping that they weren't routinely recording the phone calls from the outside to the guard room.

'I don't know how to do it, but I want to plead insanity,' I told her.

She was quiet for a moment.

'Are you still there?' I asked.

'Yes, I am here but … are you sure?' she said slowly.

'Yes, but someone else has to do it for me.' Luckily the guards gave me a bit of privacy for a call with my mother, because this was the first time I had said out loud the idea that had been fermenting in my mind. I hadn't even told Carl. 'I can't fight them from here with no money, and they are going to lock me up for ten years.'

'All right,' she said. 'I'll see what I can do, but remember what I always told you when you were just a little boy walking to school: let Divine Light be your guidance.' She was still a Christian then, long before she became a Buddhist and learnt to live in the moment.

I thought it best not to tell her that I planned to plead insanity so as to get into some place that I could reasonably hope to escape from.

Apart from these brief moments of contact, I was completely isolated from the world outside.

Prayer number 428:
Somebody please be on my side … there is nothing more powerless than being locked up with no control and the knowledge that there is nobody out there working for you. The cold, lonely depression. All of the futility angels show up in droves and you just want to slash your wrists. There is no way out. Walls. Guns. Locks. No hope. The only way is to turn informer in some way or other … somebody please be on my side.

One day I was called out from my cell and told that there was a visitor for me downstairs. They said it was my girlfriend. Girlfriend? I didn't have a girlfriend. Not that I knew of. A guard took me down in the lift from the fourth floor to the ground floor, where they had visiting rooms off to the side behind the main charge office, and who should I find there but Bridget, Bridget-fucking-H, my crazy jol-to-the-max friend with whom I'd lived in the house up on the slopes of the mountain back in Cape Town. The last time I'd seen her we had shared a couple of shots of Jack Daniel's and a pot of coffee in the morning while waiting for Donny to pick me up.

Bridget had come. Not my grandfather or my rowdy, gun-toting cousins (I should be so lucky) or my siblings; not my best friend, my rock 'n' roll band or my Long Street brothers ... but Bridget. Bridget knew where I'd been and what I was doing, and somehow she had discovered what had happened to me.

And she had come for me.

Girls weren't in the same zone as boys. When boys are young, the girls get their period, the blood shows up, and no amount of wishing can change the reality of life. They learnt early. Later, when the boys were seventeen or so, they had to pick up the gun, and the girls had to stand on the side and cheer as their brothers and boyfriends got blooded. The girls weren't called to kill. When they got the blood it was the sign of life, of the next generation. Which is more daunting: to bring life into this world or to terminate it?

Did Bridget even relate to, or understand, the quandary I was in before I landed in the shit, all that stuff about Peace, Love and Apartheid, the Army, my Mathological Equations? The thing is, it didn't really matter. What mattered was that she was on my side, and just knowing that someone is doing some little thing for you, and that you are not yet sentenced to the eternal lonely night – that little thought can give you strength when you have no power to act for yourself.

The world outside was full of people who just wanted money, or sex, always to be the winner, people who would tolerate any kind of shit, averting their eyes from injustice and brutality, so they could have a swimming pool and a Mercedes-Benz. This world where there was no honour, no romance, no trust. Just stinking little humans waddling in the excrement of their desires. And she, one fucked-up human on the Highway to Hell, comes to give me hope.

From hopelessness to hope. It is a fantastic journey. A beautiful gift. I will love that girl forever. Hope can give you strength, can make you dare to dream.

When the guard took me to the visiting room, I couldn't believe it. Bridget, sweet Bridget, looking so damn pleased with herself – triumphant, in fact. It was her favourite emotion, I think. Back in Cape Town she'd been angry as hell at me, giving me shit because I wanted to go to sleep early and not party with her friends. Man, she was one angry girl sometimes. She was the last person I'd have thought would be visiting. It was one hundred per cent surprise. I was stunned. Until then she had always been a Cape Town girl, but there she was, in John Vorster Square, like some necromancer bitch stepping into the cold concrete Afterworld of what was once my life, my Recent-Life Experience, telling me that there was a way out. *Don't give up. Don't die. We will not forget you.*

Had she come to Joburg especially for me? I choose to believe so, and I don't mean that she came for love, but because I was a friend who needed help, though I sometimes wonder if perhaps she just got too big for Cape Town and was going to be in Joburg anyway. Everyone in South Africa ends up in the City of Gold at some time or other, some in search of the gold, others just to survive.

She was bullying a small group of policemen who were grovelling before her like puppies, and when she turned to me she had the most amazing smug expression on her face. At age seventeen she was discovering that her powers of control over men knew no bounds. She gave me a hug like she was my girlfriend and she slipped three sticks of Durban Poison in my waistband and then gave me a kiss. I had never kissed Bridget before and, using her tongue, she pushed a bunch of pills into my mouth. She knew that I didn't do that stuff, but I could trade it for cigarettes.

'Hi Bridget,' I mumbled, my mouth full of Mandrax and Obex. I had to keep them hidden there for at least twenty minutes until I returned to my cell, but both varieties were hard pills that could be tucked into a corner of my mouth without dissolving.

'Oh you big stupid,' she laughed.

It seemed they were all in town, Bridget, Ess, Jay and others. From what I could make out, Bridget had rented offices and was running a 'massage parlour', as they were known then, specialising in 'pelvic massage'. Madame Bridget, right out of the wildest Western. She had put a fleet of girls together and brought the act to the Big City. Bridget and the Pussy Posse coming to fuck me out of jail!

I try to imagine the world through her eyes. To me, I was here and over there were these evil motherfuckers defined in evilness by their badges and their uniforms, their blind obedience to stupidity and their callous enjoyment of their power. But perhaps to her they, me, we, we were all just guys, men who could be used and manipulated by their penises or, even better, their numbskull brains. It was a strange mixture, you know?

Power politics. Gender politics. Sex politics.

The men could stand in opposite teams, facing each other with swords – fascists, communists, black, white – but to women they could all be viewed as possible mates, dates, tricks, people to be used as steps to power. The same way that some men would rate women, hire or fire them, based on whether or not they looked sexy in heels rather than on their ability and intelligence.

After being stuck there so long in that cold cell, with winter coming on hard through the metal mesh, I was lonely. Nobody was trying to help me with legal matters besides my mother, who was more than a thousand kilometres away.

My brother never came to Joburg. My father never came to Joburg. My uncles never came to Joburg, but my aunt came and I remember that. My aunt and Bridget and her gang of Outlaw Chicks. (Where would this sad world be without Distant Aunts and Outlaw Chicks?)

When Bridget turned up, I was in a deep hole of denial and despair, and I had no access at all to any real hands-on help. Not even a lawyer pretending to help. Just me sitting and waiting while my mother made long-distance phone calls. Bridget turned up and she told me she had come to help, not just visit. She was from home, from the warm south.

THE UNEXPLODED BOER

All the other visits I received, they were gone in a flash. When my aunt came she was there for about one minute, if that, and the same went for the visits from Derek. All they were allowed was time to hand me my gifts, wish me good luck and leave.

But Bridget came every day. She brought me everything I needed. Chickens and chocolate and money and dagga. She brought hope and possibilities. We laughed together like it was nothing, nothing we couldn't handle. The police wanted her to stay longer; they would do anything to please her if it meant that she would come again soon and focus her shining energy upon them once more. She seemed to have no limits and I almost had a heart attack every time she showed up, but the boys in blue couldn't get enough of her.

Until then I had always thought that men in uniform were people who wanted power, who lived to give orders, to strut around, but in her presence they showed another side. I realised that men in uniform more than anything want to take orders, be obedient and receive approval. They want to be told what to do.

Bridget would bring me hot steaming barbecue chickens that stank up the whole of John Vorster Square, driving people into a frenzy. Stuffed inside was all a guy could ask for besides freedom. I told her she shouldn't bring me any more contraband because they were starting to search prisoners, so she used the chickens as drug mules. She said I needed representation, a legal team with briefcases. She would get the money for a lawyer from her 'massage business' (and who knows what else she was up to). She was not the most subtle operator on the block, though, and soon attracted the attention of the vice squad, so she immediately started dating the vice squad officer.

Her view of the world was so different. She just dated the cop. Me, I viewed the cop as a representative of the government, the police state outreach programme of control, violence and evil. I had these idiotic fantasies about connections and linkages and cause-and-effect theories. She dated the cop. Did she fuck him, set him up with a girl, or just dazzle him and leave him panting on a ledge? Oh, she was something else. Trouble with a capital T, but Trouble with a heart full of soul.

When Bridget couldn't visit, she sent other beautiful girls, and I became famous for the delicious young women who came to the prison, their perfumes and powders, satin blouses and tight denim jeans briefly charging the air with transient fantasies. Outside in the free world, guys I had never met became 'interested' in my situation because of the sexy girls who flocked to town, and there was always some cat with a hot motorcycle or a souped-up set of wheels ready to ferry my visitor of the day. Bridget had power by the throat and she was determined to dig me out of my hole with the ferocity of a dog digging out the last rabbit in the universe. She was the staunchest connection a loser could have.

A lot of people could learn from her ...

★★★★★★★★★★★ 19 ★★★★★★★★★★★

INSANITY

A few days after Bridget's first visit there were some interesting new additions to the prison population. First there were three kids, boys who looked to be between eleven and fourteen, who were put in one of the cells on their own in the general holding area. They had run away from some kind of home.

Things were wild then, with heavy drinking by guards and prisoners alike, and crazy shit started to happen. The kids had girls coming to visit them in the contact rooms downstairs and these girls smuggled them hacksaw blades just like in the movies, and they cut through the bars of their cells and, unknown to everybody, crept around the prison at night.

Me and Carl would hang and talk philosophy with the half-baked guards and things were generally sloppy. Sometimes, after supper when the night-shift staff had got their mugs going good, this black dude would signal me from the end of the white prisoners' hallway and I would sneak around the corner to the 'black' section for a drink and a smoke, because things were so lax the guards sometimes didn't lock the gates that separated our colour-coded sections of the floor.

It was just the way it was then, as it is now, with young people refusing to follow the dictates of their elders. I wasn't from Johannesburg and hadn't had any significant contact with the people of the area apart from Samson and his lady friend at the house. There were black people everywhere, driving and carrying and sweeping and guarding and delivering, so it's not that they were invisible. They were visible everywhere. In Johannesburg it seemed to me that the white people did the actual living while all these other people ran around organising and maintaining their lives for them.

In the popular media stereotype, the black prisoners would have been 'tsotsis', dangerous to everybody, especially white guys. I wonder which stereotype I would have been. And what kind of idiots were we anyway, all of us, locked up for who knows what stupid things, still somehow managing to turn the moment into an occasion for a drink and a smoke?

Smoking pipes and drinking liquor in the bathroom of the black section of John Vorster Square, an apartheid nightmare, all of us going down to some hell or other. We stopped for some light chatter and to communicate, shake hands and exchange the long-arm clasp of the street.

'If I don't see you through the week ...'

'I'll see you through the window ...'

'My *blaaah*.'

While Carl and I enjoyed some sort of privacy from the regular hurly-burly, the stink, hustle and angst of the holding cells, we also tended to miss some of the new arrivals. It was a nasty business watching groups of people being brought in, because they were always in shock, depressed and unhappy, drawn as they usually were from a life of deprivation and bureaucratic victimisation. Then the guards would humiliate them in front of everyone, verbally abusing them and threatening them with violence.

Naturally the white prisoners got the light treatment. When black prisoners arrived they got the full colonial dressing down, and the nastiest men relished the moment as they strode like sergeant majors shouting, screaming at some poor kid, some terrified family man. *Fokken kaffer! Kaffer! Kaffer!* They didn't just threaten violence; they used actual violence and smugly threatened further dark brutality should the prisoner show any signs of resistance. Resistance was futile, and often fatal.

We didn't often see this hands-on application of apartheid in the English society of the Cape. People there liked to pretend that this kind of thing didn't happen, that it wasn't commonplace and definitely wasn't the cornerstone, the most vital foundation of the whole economic empire. One-on-one violence.

There were some big white men in South Africa, who one would come across now and then. Men with bodies like barrels, who could conceivably wrestle a bull by the horns and force it to the ground, and they usually had nicknames like 'Tiny' or 'Bubbles'. Boetman was related to them, I think, because he was a biggie.

There was one big guy who I met in a forlorn and decrepit residential suburb way out on the south side of Joburg, a *breker*, a wide boy, a big bull-tossing, crazy-as-hell motherfucker with the wildest manic mind, who ran some backyard shebeen-cum-chop-shop. Endicott's brother's flatmate had taken me to his place of business a day or two before I was arrested, and I may have sold him some *gif*, or tried to, but he was totally erratic and just plain psycho. Just trying to have a straight conversation with him was a nightmare and I thought he was stark-raving bonkers and got away from him as quickly as possible, but he was, for sure, an eminently memorable, manic monster man who spoke in a stream-of-consciousness flow, a patter of Jozi argot, that was hypnotic and lulling. Sometimes I find it hard to tell the genius from the madman.

I'd always thought that the Cape Town Afrikaans patois, with its mixture of accents and languages, was the most colourful in the country, but I had become totally enamoured with the wide, flamboyant working-class Johannesburg accent. Anyway, while sharing a cup of 'coffee' with the guards one evening (yet another strange arrangement that Carl's silver tongue and winning ways had facilitated) I

INSANITY

heard a long torrent of verbal abuse coming down the corridor of the holding cells, starting with a loud 'Listen, my china', and I thought I recognised that insane prison poetry resounding off the walls. I walked out of the guard's room and saw him, just two cells down on the right, his big fists gripping the bars of the cage as he harangued some old connection in another cell across the way.

'Ag, come on my *boet*, shoot me a *entjie asseblief*,' he pleaded to his friend. '*Ek het niks hier.*'

'*Nay man*,' came the reply, '*ek ook ou maat. Ons is nou saam diep in'ie kak.*'

The big guy turned his head and saw me watching him with a mug of brandy-flavoured coffee in one hand and a cigarette dangling from my mouth, and I thought he recognised me from our earlier encounter.

'Hey, cool cat,' he called softly to me, bringing his hand to his mouth and miming a satisfying pull on a cigarette.

We were in a delicate situation with the night-shift guards, and even I realised that it would not be wise to abuse their hospitality, at least not until they were really loaded. Going down that hallway and chatting to prisoners was a definite no-no at that early hour, so I took two Texans from my pack and shot them across the floor to him, receiving a thumbs-up and a wink in return. As I turned to rejoin Carl and the two guards in their deep debate I saw Bull Tosser, in turn, slide one of the smokes across to his friend in the other cell.

Somehow, out of all the people in the huge city, we were there in the same place. I wondered if his arrest had anything to do with me. I wondered if the police had followed me and lost me in the traffic, as Boetman had claimed, but only after I had visited his establishment. The timing would have been right. Maybe they followed me to him and returned at a later date to knock him over. I felt guilty.

It was only Carl and me who had been raised to the status of guard 'guests', and the only interaction we had with other inmates was when they brought us food. Usually two guys carried the food, escorted by a guard.

So one night the big Bull Tosser brought the food to our cell in a big pot, a huge three-legged *potjie* with *stompie* legs. Man, that guy was big. Another prisoner slopped the food on the tin plates. The big guy looked down at me, lifting the monster-sized pot with one hand like he was going hit me with it. Then he burst into a high-pitched giggle and slapped me on the back with his free hand, sending me lurching into the arms of the cop, who pushed me away in disgust.

'*Fok* him, ha ha ha.' He swung the big pot around, making all three of us jump back in alarm. '*Fok* him! *Fok* Boetman. *Jou ma se moer!*' he roared gleefully at the top of his lungs. 'No, I won't do it. He fuck me up, got me for a parcel, yiss man. All I got to do is *moer* you *sat* and I go home one-time *ek sê*, but I like you. I like you. So fuck him.'

Then they left, with the nervous cop keeping a healthy distance from the pot-wielding giant. As they walked down the grey concrete corridor, the sound of the keys jangling in the hand of their escort, echoing eternally, the big guy turned around and aimed his forefinger at me, shot a little electric bolt at my third eye. Zap!

Once more he bellowed, '*Fok* you, *jou ma se moer, jou befokte boer!*' He was still giggling as they disappeared round the corner.

It appeared to me, from what the Bull Tosser had said, that he must have been a convenient madman for Boetman, who had gone and rousted him just to get him in the prison, busting him with just enough to make him face 'dealing' charges and then offering to drop all charges if he would 'take care' of me. But he didn't go through with the arrangement. Life is strange sometimes.

Using their smuggled hacksaw blades, the three little boys cut through the bars of the door to a back set of stairs and over time made their way down two more floors. There they found a window to the outside world and cut out the bars, tied their blankets together and escaped from John Vorster Square. They stole a policeman's personal car from outside the station complex and went and totalled it, driving it through a wall into somebody's house.

Their idea was fabulous, audacious and almost magnificent. Those children dared to try and almost succeeded, but it all went completely wrong for them. The police brought them back to John Vorster Square and beat and kicked and beat and beat till there was nothing left but whimpering blood. Then they put them in some place where no one could see them till they healed. All kinds of major kak came down over that escape, and the slovenly drunk who was in charge that night lost his job. New people came in and security was tightened up.

My mother finally managed to get another call through to me, and she told me that she had indeed reached the chief prosecutor and had had two 'very nice' conversations with the man, who was 'quite understanding'. She told him that I had always had problems dealing with school and life in general and how drugs seemed to have changed my mind for the worse, emphasising the fact that I wasn't violent and had no criminal history, juvenile or otherwise, and she was so worried because my seemingly harmless paternal grandfather had been incarcerated in Valkenberg after a psychotic episode which resulted in his shooting a total stranger. Even though the doctors assured her that this wasn't a hereditary condition ... well, you just never know. All in all she convinced him that I was very possibly psychologically bonkers (she may have believed that too?) and that a plea of insanity should be put forward. Did I mention that my mother won the Most Promising Actress award at age sixteen back in 1939?

Before my next court appearance, the guard told me to bring my personal effects with me. I still had nothing but the clothes I'd been arrested in and some cigarettes. Carl and me, we had been through some things. We drank a lot of brandy, smoked a lot of cigarettes and had conversations about every subject under the sun at every hour of the day and night. We had been pissed off at each other and made one another laugh. We shook hands and made a simple farewell pact.

'If you don't come back tonight, I'll see you on the outside, *bru*,' he said.

'On the outside,' I repeated.

That morning I was one of the eager guys with a gleam in his eye riding in the court-bound truck. My plan was in motion and I was looking forward to some change in my otherwise bleak future. We were once again marched underneath the courts to wait our turn on the stage, but this time there were no choruses of men singing Pink Floyd songs, just the murmur of muted conversations and clouds of smoke, as men paced back and forth smoking nervously. Winter was coming on hard and it was bitterly cold down there, but one of Bridget's girls who had taken a serious liking to me made the early-morning trek before going to work and brought me a long denim coat, which she was allowed to give me.

She put her soft hands through the bars and held my face for a moment before leaving. Once again I felt just how sacred the human touch can be.

My court appearance, as usual, was nothing spectacular. I walked up from the feeder room and stood in the box, nervous as hell, as the beady-eyed old judge looked my scruffy person over. The black-garbed prosecutor stood up like a bent crow and told the judge that he was recommending that I be remanded to The Fort, an ancient prison in the heart of Johannesburg, for assessment by the prison doctor, who would decide whether I should be sent to a sanatorium for twenty-eight days' observation to determine whether or not I was mentally competent to stand trial and be held accountable for my misdeeds. The gavel came down with a crack and I was advanced to the next round. I have to admit I was feeling quite mad and getting madder every moment.

I needed to get out of jail (duh!). All the time I had that one thought in my head. From the beginning, the mission was to escape the country. The mission was still escape, but it was now just a little more obvious.

And a little more complicated.

THE FORT

The holding area in John Vorster Square was a chaotic mess compared to The Fort, which was a prison run not by policemen but by the prison service, and they operated with discipline and routine and an organised network of smuggling and corruption. Back in the real world. No more fuck-head cops.

It was another place, another place to be broken into little bits and categorised and stamped and reduced to the most basic level of existence. At least there were no more midnight question sessions, but that would change the following year when the troubles began. They would be torturing people everywhere, all pretence of civility abandoned as they revelled in their apocalyptic fury.

The first things the new custodians wanted to know were our names and the charges against us. Then we were led through big gates and small gates and deeper into the Stonewarden's Palace. The guard turned to me.

'Hey Rautenbach, I hope you're not an escape artist.' He raised his eyebrows quizzically, but in good humour, as he pointed to the side of a building where a thin ladder-like set of stairs snaked up to the second floor, where a heavy door was set in the wall. 'We have a relative of yours up there, another Rautenbach, who's escaped so many times that we have to keep him up there. He just won't give up and he gets deeper in kak all the time.'

I had an ancient cell, maybe eight by eight feet, with pitted and pockmarked wooden floors, which I shared with a guy who seemed overly eager for new company, especially if it came with cigarettes. There was no toilet: we each had a tin can that we had to shit and piss into. Every morning there was an inspection, the prisoners standing to attention while the *gartjie* examined the neatly rolled grey mat, the two blankets folded one around the other to form a traditional prison 'radio', and the shiny polished floor. Standing there next to a tin can filled with urine and faeces, which was always the first smell that burned into the nostrils upon waking every morning, the overnight stench of piss. It's amazing how quickly you can get accustomed to these things. We trooped out in a line and filed one by one past a hole in the middle of the courtyard, where the can was emptied, washed under a tap and returned to the cell.

Then breakfast: a can of coffee and *katkop*, wholewheat bread with golden syrup. Three regular meals a day for the first time in ages. Of course the bedding and sleeping arrangements were much the same: the skinny grey pad and the dirty blankets. Only when you got sentenced did you actually get the haircut, the khaki prison uniform and a bed, an actual bed off the floor, as well as a tobacco ration and other minor privileges that created some small semblance of a life.

Those of us in remand got nothing but the three meals, but even that was a whole deal better than the intermittent food at John Vorster Square. I was supposed to be going to the prison hospital to be checked out, but they just left me in the regular section and I tried to survive.

I met some guys in there who I'd met in Durban Central Prison almost four years before. They didn't look so big four years later. My cellmate was a young Afrikaner thief with a troubled past who tried his hardest to turn us into good buddies right away, sharing his life with me and acting like we were brothers, but some people said he was a plant, an informer. I have no idea if he was, but he definitely asked a lot of questions. He babbled on and on about his childhood on a farm, about his teenage years in various unsavoury boys' institutions, and about his plans to escape from prison and go and live in the desert 'like a Bushman'. He claimed he knew how to find water anywhere.

There were a lot of strange characters. There were these two drag queens who had committed a series of armed robberies and were going down for twenty-five years. Nineteen years old and being locked up for a quarter of a century. The prospect was so totally unbearable to me, but they seemed casual about it, at least outwardly. Where did they come from? How could they have gone so far out? There were others too, guys going in for murder and for armed robbery, guys with long records, damning records, waiting to go down for long years.

These doomed men radiated a kind of purity. They knew where they were going and they seemed to be relieved, in a way, that the challenges of life were out of their hands ... maybe. There was a certain stillness about them that I remember. This one guy, he summoned me through some go-between to his *pozi*, where he had instant coffee and all the trimmings, and when I entered his cell he handed me a blisteringly hot enamel mug of coffee sweetened with condensed milk. He'd heard about me, he said, and the word was out that I was a *staunch connection*, one who didn't roll on his brothers in the night, one who kept the faith, the religion of the damned. He shook my hand and told me they would keep a place upstairs for me at the Big House, Pretoria Central Prison, which is where I'd most likely end up when sentenced.

The real reason that this hard exterior of muscle and stone-cold bone summoned me to his court was for words. He'd heard I was in the music business and he was looking for the words of popular songs to write in his book, an old school exercise book. Beatles, Dylan, The Archies. It didn't matter. He wanted them all. There was something childlike in the faith he placed in those words that would keep him company for the next twenty-five years.

Bridget came to visit me often and, as before, she stirred up the whole damn prison. As usual she would bring me the best barbecued roast chicken, tangy and tasty, and every day the whole prison would reek of my chicken as men begged and called to me while others sang the praises of fine women. Her presence was a hornet's nest as she roused everything and everyone into a nervous energy. She was loud and gregarious and flirtatious and downright abusive and sexual. She burnt too much petrol always.

We would talk through the wire mesh, laughing and joking, and I'd boast about the wonderful place and all the fabulous meals we were having and the ice-cream parfait desserts. We engaged in the repartee of fools, talking between the lines in a fantasy of bravado, a great pretend world that lesser beings could only marvel at, that other people who believed in everything, in God, Country and all the little stories, could only dimly comprehend. We were a comic book of tears painted in spandex.

There was one young guard, so religious and very, very tense. He really wanted to help me. After Bridget had dropped by and we'd had our party through the wire, talking loudly and flamboyantly so the guards and inmates and visitors could hear and see us, he would pull me aside and tell me that I really had to get *serious*.

'You are in a lot of trouble,' he would tell me as he escorted me back to my cell. 'You have to take your situation seriously.'

'I have no idea what you're talking about,' I replied. I can't really say why I was playing this game with him. It just seemed the thing to do.

'Your life is ruined, can't you see?'

'No, it's not. I'm having a fantastic time.' I bounced along with a skip in my step and a smile on my face.

'No!' He stopped and glared at me. 'You are in prison and you will be sentenced for a long time. You have to be serious.'

Then Bridget would visit again and the guard would take me to see her. Each time he got more and more agitated by my complete refusal to understand words like 'problem' and 'deep trouble'. And

Bridget drove him demented. She would sit there dressed for sex, with little lapdogs that used to be men rolling on their backs at her command.

The poor guard would stand there sweating as this Whore of Babylon performed for the amazed visitors and inmates. We would joke and talk about the high life, the champagne, the beautiful weather and the wonderful music, always agreeing that life was too good to be true, and exclaiming how wonderful the guards were and how fabulous the food was.

Eventually, I heard, that poor guard had a very public emotional breakdown and was transferred somewhere else.

21

THE FORT HOSPITAL

After waiting a few weeks in the regular remand section of The Fort, I was finally transferred from my cell to the 'hospital', which was one room with four beds. They must have been waiting for a bed to become free for me ... maybe somebody died.

There were three other 'patients'. One was a tough, wiry guy called Eric, about fifty years of age, who told me he had been running from the police in Woodstock in Cape Town and ran straight into the traffic and was hit by a truck that crushed his leg. The leg had been amputated, but not his spirit or his sense of humour. He was a career jailbird.

At first glance Eric looked to me like an old legless guy with deep lines etched around his mouth and eyes, but I learnt very quickly that he had this unstoppable mischievous rebel spirit and a motivational mania that converted every coming moment into a fresh opportunity. He relished the next altercation, the next collision of calamities, and he never looked back in anger or regret. Also, he knew my new world inside and out, all the gossip and scandals about prisoners and guards. He knew exactly what was what but he never toed the line.

'You got to take it a year at a time, a year at a time,' he told me, 'especially when you're doing a Coat.' *Doing a Coat* was slang for the sentence called 'nine-to-fifteen' (years) but known in the prison community as a 'coat of arms'. Heavy, heavy clothing. Eric claimed to have done two Coats. *'n Ou aap van die Kaap.*

A year at a time! I was only twenty. A day was sometimes an eternity to me.

The second patient was about seventy and he too had only one leg. This rapscallion pensioner had been caught repeatedly for possession of marijuana, so they'd locked him up for three years to 'teach him a lesson'.

Next to these one-legged, arrogant, noisy, foul-mouthed and bedridden jesters, the third patient was a small mouse of a man. He'd just sit quietly in his bed while I joked around with the other two or spent hours doing yoga and standing on my head. His crime was that he'd purchased things on credit and then claimed not to remember having done so. He was pleading amnesia.

Eric was a real 'bad boy' but a very good man. It's funny how those two so often coincide. He was some kind of perpetual robber on the wrong side of the law, but without guys like him the rest of us would die of boredom in hospitals and armies. He was always smoking weed and in constant battle with a mean-spirited guard who he called the 'blind spy'. This guard would sneak up and burst into the room, and when he did, everyone was supposed to jump up and stand at attention next to their beds, especially one-legged men.

I had still not seen a doctor or been informed of what was going on. I didn't have a lawyer, so I got no updates or briefs. I was still wearing the same pair of jeans that I'd been arrested in, bleached out and covered in patches. One of Bridget's girls had brought me needles and coloured embroidery thread so I could mend them where they were falling apart, and using the extensive time on my hands I fashioned a huge marijuana plant climbing all the way up my left leg. She also brought me two beautifully illustrated hard-cover editions of Conan the Barbarian, which were quickly passed on to other inmates and became part of the underground prison library.

My twenty-first birthday was coming up – 16 June 1975, one year before the terrible revolution began, so many families torn apart. Bridget told me she was going to arrange a special surprise for me.

THE UNEXPLODED BOER

On the morning of my birthday I was taken from the hospital cell all the way to the head warden, the boss of the prison. He had the telephone in his hand.

'It's your mother,' he said.

My mother! I grabbed the phone and it was her. She'd called to wish me a very happy twenty-first birthday. Fuck! Why bother? I suppose she wanted to let me know that she was thinking of me, but the irony! Didn't she get it? I could hear the wry note in her voice – that hospital voice that people use when they look at you lying on your back with tubes going in and out of your body.

'Happy birthday, darling, I hope you get everything you wished for.' She was already a secret agent speaking in code. I knew she was referring obliquely to my insanity plea.

'Oh yes, things are already much better. I'm in the hospital now and I even have a real bed with nice clean sheets, which is a big improvement. Even the food is better. It's like a fancy hotel,' I joked.

'Well, I hope they don't charge you too much,' she countered, following my lead.

'No, it's not too steep. All they want is five years of my life and a piece of my soul.'

'Well, you just remember that you are God's perfect creation and he has a plan for you,' she replied, always finding a way to slide in the God business.

In my mother's colonial English culture, twenty-one was the 'age of majority', and on that birthday your father traditionally gave you the key to the front door. Birthday cards were always adorned with the key motif, a silver key that looked a whole lot like the keys that prison guards kept on a big ring as they walked around with their jangle jangle. It was supposed to be the biggest party of your life to date.

'I would like to wish you all the best, son, under the circumstances,' offered the prison boss, 'and if there is anything special I can do for you …' His eyebrows rose slightly in fatherly command. I just couldn't resist.

'Well, sir, it *is* my twenty-first birthday, so if you could give me

THE FORT HOSPITAL

the key to the front door, I would be really happy.' I gave him what I hoped was an open and honest smile. He didn't crack. Not a smidgen. He just looked at me with that baleful stare, as if he had made a genuine offer and I had rubbed it in the dirt.

Fuck you, I thought to myself. Fuck you all.

I was taken back to the hospital and I was still in a pissed-off mood when a guard came and called me and told me that I had another visitor, even though it wasn't visiting time.

'It's police business,' the guard said. 'Something to do with your case.' No drug squad policeman had spoken to me since the night Zip Nolan had told Boetman and his cronies to buzz off. Perhaps it had grown and grown, the way these things do, and no cop in his right mind would want to mess with the man who wore his sunglasses at night.

Sure enough I was taken into a room and handed over to a plainclothes policeman, one I had never seen before. He was carrying a file folder and he had a ratty look, like he had been up too long, jittery like a pill raver, and they let him take me out into a sealed courtyard, just the two of us between towering windowless walls for a 'private interview'.

It was a cold, dry Joburg winter's day and he wore a big overcoat. I was freezing but it was good to be outdoors. Any change was good, but I was still wondering just what the hell was going on and who this guy was.

'Listen,' he said, looking left and right as he spoke. He couldn't stand still and he shuddered and shook with pure nervous energy. 'It's your birthday, right?'

I nodded, even more puzzled, as the cop opened his overcoat and showed me the inside pocket, where he had a big bottle of Southern Comfort. It suddenly became clear to me. This was the vice squad cop who Bridget was 'dating'. He was in her thrall, at her beck and call, and she had sent him all the way on a case that wasn't his, breaking all kinds of rules and laws, to bring me a bottle of Southern Comfort on my twenty-first birthday behind the walls of The Fort.

Southern bloody Comfort. The liquor, the booze, the tragedy, the Southern rock legend, the rebel drink, the suicide sip.

'Please, please,' he implored me. 'Don't take it. Please. I brought it all the way here for you, but I could lose my job, I could lose everything. Please.'

'What's the fucking point of bringing it all the way here and not drinking it?' I teased.

I could lie to you right here. There were only the two of us out there in that courtyard. No one else will ever know what happened or if what I say really even took place.

If I was the heroic rebel, the larger-than-life swashbuckler with no regard for the consequences, then I would tell a different story. I should tell a different story, but I can't. I should say that I threw my head back and laughed a loud and hearty laugh that rang out above the roofs, and then I took that bottle and chugged a quarter of it without stopping. I would like to tell you that I toasted that crazy girl, there behind the stone walls of The Fort, forcing her useless cop to share a drink and a toast with me, then smashing the bottle against the wall and walking away.

Something like that.

But I didn't. Something had happened already. I sensed a possible chance for something if my trip to the madhouse worked out. Something. Something. I didn't know what, but I didn't want to mess it up. I was afraid, because I possibly had something to lose. So I didn't drink from that bottle. I didn't crack the seal on the golden lid. Not a single sip. But one day ... one day.

I'll never forget my twenty-first birthday, even though I didn't get the key to the front door, and I didn't get drunk. They often say it's not the gift but the thought that counts. I can sit here, all these years later, and the gift is just as fresh as it was then, because in my mind it is always a measure, a benchmark against which other actions, especially my own, can be held.

I couldn't believe it! Where do you find replacements for people

THE FORT HOSPITAL

like Bridget, friends who come through in the most amazing and imaginative ways? You don't just walk down the street and find these kinds of people; they are very few and far between in this life, and they usually don't last long on this earth.

I had a momentary pang of pity for the poor cop who had wandered into Bridget's web, and I watched him walk away with his bottle, my bottle. She probably made him pay for it too. I don't know what she had on him or what she'd done to him, but he sure was a mess. He gave me a pack of Lucky Strike cigarettes.

'Thank you, thank you,' he said, and he left me with another plea. 'Please, don't tell her.'

I eventually did see the prison doctor, who called me to his office and asked me in an offhand and uninterested manner if I was a drug addict, and I lied, telling him I used heroin, Mandrax, cocaine, morphine, LSD, hashish, yellow dexies, purple dexies, black beauties and speed, and after a few moments he sighed:

'No peyote?'

'Not yet.'

'Okay, I think you are crazy,' he said. 'You can go back to the hospital.' Then, as I exited his office, he looked up from his desk, where he was writing. 'Oh ... and good luck.' That was it, my entire interview and observation by the 'prison hospital staff'.

Derek the Taxi Driver met Bridget and gave her my black velvet suit, which she brought to me, along with my white takkies. Using the 'prison iron' technique, I carefully folded the suit and my shirt and placed them under my mattress to be pressed while I slept. A week of that and they come out immaculate. I planned to look spiffy for my next court appearance, instead of being all bedraggled and unkempt, which is how things end up when you are locked in a little room with no access to life.

I looked so good, my hair washed and shining like a surfer-boy's bleached bonny, my white satin shirt, my suit pressed beautifully by the prison iron and my takkies bright and white. I didn't wear socks, because I wasn't a businessman or a policeman. The guards told me to take everything I owned with me and I shook hands with the one-legged pirates, who wished me well.

'Remember: a year at a time,' Eric said, just before I was led off to the Monday-morning court truck. 'But if you get your chance to run, take it and don't look back, or you might run into a fucken truck like me. Never look back when you are running!'

There were quite a few people I knew among the spectators in court, and the prosecutor pointed out to the judge with a smirk that I was looking very pretty that day.

'Ja, maar hy is pragtig vandag, u Edelagbare.'

It was a special day, but I was torn between two desires. One was to stand and give a speech on record that because South Africa was an illegal rogue state, any and all judgments against me were illegitimate, and as such I did not concede that they, the system and the judge, had any authority at all.

The problem was my other, conflicting desire. I wanted to be found crazy. I wanted to go to the madhouse and escape and go far away and live happily ever after where all the nice people were. Saying something overtly 'political' might have triggered a bad reaction, cancelling my planned excursion to lunacy and inspiring some sort of patriotic zeal in my custodians, and the ensuing violence would have hurt me way more than it hurt them, believe me, plus my suit would probably have got torn and bloody. Hey, it was the only suit I had. Come to think of it, it was the only blood I had too.

Instead I played the clown and stood quietly as the judge went into a long speech in that grating Transvaal Afrikaans, on and on about some subsection, this and that. When it was over he asked me, in Afrikaans, whether I had anything to say. I smiled back and answered in English.

'I didn't understand a single word you just said. Do you think you could repeat it in English?' I don't think that it had occurred to him that someone with a good Boer name like Rautenbach could not comprehend his native language.

If I had been raised in the Boer tribe, with the language, the culture, the history, the religion and the hordes of uncles and aunts and cousins, then I would have understood all that he'd said, but I hadn't. That was a whole different reality, another life in an alternate timestream that could have happened but didn't. In that life I wouldn't be in prison in the first place.

I might have played rugby, lorded it over my servants and maids, and marched off to war with patriotic fervour, hungry to kill terrorists and communists for Jesus and the freedom of the Western world and the right to drive a Chevy Impala with a case of Castle and a box of boerewors in the boot. Though I suppose it is equally possible that I could have become a dissident Afrikaner poet and decamped to Paris to read the works of Frantz Fanon with like-minded intellectuals.

Patriotism, to me, was to be on the opposite side, a bizarre turn-about where my patriotic zeal was turned back on its own people, like some kind of renegade. But I was not a renegade; I could not renege if I had never been part of their world in the first place. They were foreign to me and their tribe was not my tribe. I had missed the boat of national Boer pride and become lumpen through circumstance, floating outside of a national paradigm, grounded in nothing but a shifting hodgepodge of native superstition, negative optimism and pure contempt.

So while I actually could understand the Taal that the judge spoke, and was only trying to be annoying, I really could not understand his society, his culture or any of the stuff that they did. I knew the history and the reasoning but I could not comprehend.

So the judge went back to the beginning and read his decision in English, going through the appropriate wording of amendment number bullshit and paragraph what-the-fuck and informing me in a cold tone that I was to be taken from the court to a place yet to be determined and hung from the neck till I was dead ... wait, wait, wait. That too was a different timestream.

In this wobbly reality, at The End of my first life, the judge went back to the beginning and told me in English, still in a cold tone, that I had been weighed up carefully by the prison doctor and found to be a few bricks shy of a load, so he was directing me to be sent to Sterkfontein Sanatorium for twenty-eight days' observation to determine whether I was mentally fit and competent to stand trial.

(Yes! Fucking yes!)

In my mind I punched the sky and did cartwheels. On the outside I showed no emotional reaction, and as he spoke I crudely turned my back on him and looked at all the people, waving and smiling like I was the Pope on tour. I saw up in the seats the guitarist Rian from El Cid's glam-rock band, who was going to journalism school, and I saw a whole section made up of Bridget's beauties plus quite a few boy groupies trailing after them.

Once court was done I was taken, not back to The Fort, but into the depressing grey of John Vorster Square and back into my old cell, where I was to await transportation to the mental hospital. Carl was no longer there. None of the old cops were there and the few I questioned claimed never to have seen or heard of him. It was lonely. Before, I had shared so much there with Carl, the books and drinking and singing and all that shit. Now it was just me, and I had to wait with the cold wind blowing through the windows. I read almost all of Leo Tolstoy's *War and Peace* in three days because they never turned the lights off. Sometimes I would harmonise with the hum of the fluorescent tubes. I had about twenty pages left when my transfer finally came through.

One day I'm going to have to finish that book ... or not.

STERKFONTEIN SANATORIUM

I was taken with the quiet man from the hospital in The Fort, the one who'd bought stuff he claimed not to remember buying. Not guilty for reasons of amnesia. He was being sent for observation too.

The amnesiac was a tiny man and we were handcuffed together. Our driver and custodian must have been at least seventy years old, and he drove his own vehicle, an old Renault. It was like we had been signed out of the prison system and handed over to this aged part-time courier who ferried us into some other paperwork file. This was as close as I'd come to freedom. We were out, outside, sitting in the back of a car with this spindly old duffer driving carefully out of the city, and I seriously considered reaching over and strangling him with the cuffs, forcing him to pull over, but I didn't. I was such a fucking lightweight! Scruples! Morals! Anchors of doom.

We stopped at Baragwanath Hospital in Soweto and picked something up and then headed out into the countryside. I kept on thinking about escape, tied to Memory Man, wondering if the old guy had a gun. I kept quiet, all the time aware that this might be the only chance I ever got. Then we arrived at the sanatorium out in the middle of nowhere, to me, way out of the city in the bundu on the way to Pretoria.

After driving up and down through the hills of the sunny winter countryside, we made a left turn into the entrance to Sterkfontein, two concrete posts flanked by a low stone wall that disappeared in both directions. As we drove down the entrance road I realised that this was more like a village. To our left was a host of different-sized buildings and private residences for staff, all intertwined with quaint winding streets. On our right were individual compounds, free-standing buildings, each surrounded by a high wire fence topped with barbed wire tilted inwards to prevent easy climbing.

The compounds were all named after the stations on the Cape Town railway line: Woodstock, Observatory, Mowbray and so on. My gaze was attracted by another multi-storey building, much larger than the compounds, like a small version of Valkenberg, situated about a half a kilometre away at the bottom of the valley. It had no fence or barbed wire. I was thinking how nice it was to see no gun towers and wondering whether the station names went all the way to the end of the line, to Simon's Town, when the courier pulled up in front of one of the compounds before I could read the name, but I think it was Rosebank. It was the end of the line for me.

We were ushered through the compound door into a waiting room of sorts, where a uniformed woman was writing in a book. A very prim and proper Afrikaner tannie was waiting there, her frilly lace collar tight around her neck, her hands firmly clasped around her purse, a nice lady who had no doubt come to do some good for a relative. Sunlight played through the curtains as we waited for our presence to be acknowledged.

Before that could happen, a large bear of a man with bloodless white skin and orange hair prematurely thinning over herds of freckles, dressed in pyjamas and holding his white bandaged hands directly in front of him like Frankenstein's monster, came shambling around the corner, mumbling some sort of drug-induced poetry.

'Grreagh, ghghghgh orreorrghg ...'

The guttural sound dribbled from his mouth as he went. He shuffled along in a strange side-to-side gait, as if he were dragging a dinosaur tail, straight up to the waiting tannie, who stood there staring at him, her mouth opening in a silent O, and he grabbed both her breasts in his bandaged fists. She began screaming and his gurgling became more insistent, orderlies and nurses ran in shouting, legs and feet dislodged bookshelves and vases and paintings, and then the man screamed a long, lonely howl.

'Aaaaaaaaaaaaaaaaaachchchhhh!'

I stood there open-mouthed, in total awe, as furniture crashed to the ground and two men in white wrestled with Frankenstein and they slipped to the floor amidst the broken glass, blood and scattered ornaments. The woman was still screaming as more aides arrived to drag the poor psycho away down the passage.

'Rrrgaaasshsh ... aaaaaaaaaaagh! Aaaaagh ... rrrr!'

Another woman appeared and gently soothed the screaming woman, managing to reduce her sound to a gentle whimper.

'There, there, just sit here. We'll get you some tea.' She looked up and saw the three of us standing in the doorway. 'Aaaaah – you must be the new arrivals. Welcome to Sterkfontein.'

Jirre Jissus in sy befokte moer!

The old man signed us over and took his handcuffs back and looked very happy to get the hell out of there. The receptionist summoned an orderly to see us to our new digs. It was like all places of incarceration, where new arrivals are a brief distraction from the tedium of confinement, and, as we walked down the corridors, I was very aware of the inquisitive stares from the inmates. I got the feeling that there were some crazy, crazy people in there and I was wondering just what new kak I had landed myself in.

We arrived at a dormitory that looked like some Victorian workhouse, high ceilings, a cavernous hall with dozens and dozens of beds. Institution all the way. The room had large windows the size of doors, all covered with the same metal grille as the windows at John Vorster Square, but with glass to keep out the winter cold. We were each assigned a bed and left there to fend for ourselves. I put away my belongings in the two drawers of the table beside my bed:

my velvet suit, satin shirt and the still unfinished copy of *War and Peace*. Once again I would be sleeping raised off the ground with real sheets and pillows. Things were looking up in the sleeping department. A few people came over and talked to me, mostly to see if I had cigarettes, which I did, with half a dozen packs hidden away under my suit. I lay on the bed and whiled away the time until the supper bell sounded, and I followed the crowd out onto a covered stoep with windows which served as the dining room.

I sat at the table I was assigned to with a man whose name was Dagga, who would sit all day long using a pair of pliers to insert the little metal triangle into the rubber plugs for kitchen sinks. He had been doing this for twenty-five years. Across from Dagga sat a little fellow who ate only with a spoon.

'They don't give me a knife,' he smiled cheerily, 'because I just go crazy, you know?'

Were they fucking with me?

After supper I followed the crowd to a big room where lots of the men hung around on chairs and couches, reading, drinking coffee and talking. I met a hippy there who I knew. He had flipped out and was living on Signal Hill in Cape Town the last time I'd seen him, carrying a horse's saddle over his shoulder like a cowboy walking through the desert after his horse had died.

At night a girl of about sixteen appeared at the window of the common area and most of the men rushed closer. Apparently she did this every night, flirting with everybody with her rampant innocent sexuality and that pretty little frock she wore. Someone told me she had killed her whole family, but she could walk around the grounds freely, without any escort.

'It's a privilege you earn, when they know you won't run away.'

I learnt too that some compounds had no fence around them, and that these housed the patients who were allowed to roam and who were given some responsibility. They understood their mental conditions and worked hard to get better. They were called 'trustees'.

STERKFONTEIN SANATORIUM

There was a snooker table in the centre of the common room. It was the focal point of all psychological activity. Everybody was humming with some mania, some crazy idea, some freaky thought, and the leaders, the ones who ruled at the snooker table, could switch a madman on with the right word.

They understood 'madness'. As soon as I walked in they started grilling me, asking where I came from, who I was, why I was there ... playing mind games, saying crazy things, uttering trigger words, trying to see which branch of madness I had, to see if they could break me down ...

Then another fellow (why do I always get ox-sized crazy men?) came up and said to them that he was my pal and ordered them to leave me alone. He told me he had killed his best friend with a screwdriver, thrown his shoe at the judge and got 'made mad', but then he'd killed someone with a sack of cement, so they locked him up for good.

'Nice to meet you too,' I mumbled.

'Don't worry, nobody will fuck with you if you are my friend,' he promised me.

At night there were noises and I didn't open my eyes when someone crept up and felt under my pillow for cigarettes. To say that I was afraid would be an understatement. There seemed to be no end to the possible disasters that could occur. I had to prove that I was crazy to stay out of prison, but the problem was that craziness meant getting put away in a place like Sterkfontein for 'five to fifty years – at the President's pleasure'. The other option was to escape.

I wasn't the only one with the urge to run. In the mornings we were allowed out into the yard where tea was served under a big tree, and this one guy kept freaking out and trying to climb the fence. But it was too high, and they would pull him down, hands bleeding from the barbed wire that bent in at the top, and drag him away to be sedated.

I met another young guy, a blond-headed Czechoslovakian who had some ailment or other. I called him Nutso.

The interesting thing about Nutso was that, after some prompting, he revealed to me that he had already escaped three times. *Really now?* That's why he was in the security zone with the fence.

'It's fucken cool, man,' he told me, 'you can just do anything you want and they send you back here. Anything you like!'

After a bit more prompting he told me that the last time he got away was from this very compound, by cutting the fence, but he had tied the wire strands back together so carefully that the authorities never discovered the hole.

'You mean it's still there?'

'Yes.'

'Where?'

'I can't tell you.'

'Why?'

'I'm saving it for the next time.'

Fuck. Could I really believe this cat? Nutso. But he liked me and I was going to stay his friend. I was young and cool and he wanted to be my friend. And I had to dodge the big dude, my other friend, who was very weird with anyone who talked to me. This was not fun. No.

A school contingent came by one afternoon on a 'field trip'. There we were, all the fucking crazy people who weren't strapped down, drugged out or getting electroshock therapy somewhere, and this schoolteacher comes through, escorted by Matron and Doctor and followed by about thirty teenage girls in blue skirts and white shirts, oozing teenage charm and sexuality, all legs and thighs and jutting breasts, into this den of rapists, sodomisers and suicidal masturbators. At least at the zoo they keep the children on the other side of the bars, away from the animals. It was too strange. I needed to leave. I had to leave. I knew that Bridget was working hard at getting a lawyer to work my case, but I had no faith in the system at all. I was guilty, after all, and I couldn't imagine a favourable outcome.

On my second day there, I was sent for tests with the electro-encephalograph and a coloured light show, and I sat there pushing a pin into my skin, trying to skew the results, and almost jumping from the seat with the pain. This 'trustee' took me for the tests. He checked me out of my little fortress and, armed with nothing but a clipboard, escorted me through the village-like area, reminiscent of the island where Patrick McGoohan was kept in the sci-fi television series *The Prisoner*.

I could have just run down the road between the buildings and be gone. The thought was breathtakingly inspiring, but was this the best moment? *Will there ever be another one, another moment to run?* The problem is, once you make your break you are marked as a runner, so when you go you better go good because it might be your last – your one and only – chance. The Last Chance? Is this it? I played games with the trustee.

'Hey,' I asked him, 'what would you do if I ran away?'

'I would have to tell somebody.'

'You wouldn't chase me?'

'I don't know.'

'Why don't *you* run away?'

'I can't. They trust me. I am getting better.'

'If I ran away, could you wait five minutes before telling them?'

'I don't know.'

'Would you chase me?'

'Yes ... I have to.' He looked disturbed as I kept offering him more possibilities than his recently reconstructed headspace could handle.

On my fourth day, during mid-morning teatime, I was hanging with Nutso in the yard, gently pumping him about the hole in the fence. I didn't like the vibe of the whole place, the psychos walking around at night, crazy murderers being possessive buddies, and the possibility of being there for decades. It was urgent. After four weeks they were going to send me back to prison. Freedom was my goal. Fuck Them All was my mantra. I couldn't sit around.

Nutso and me. We were out there having tea and biscuits under a clear winter sky in the old Transvaal and I asked him again where the hole in the fence was. I had to know, and finally he crumbled under my gently insistent pressure. He casually led me away from the tea table under the tree. Dispersing and conversing, an already familiar sight to observers: Nutso and the New Guy walking together. We sidled down to this little brick hut at the corner of the yard, possibly some water pump or electrical affair, and we walked behind it, out of sight of the tea table, and not visible from the stoep with the wide peeling red stairs.

'It's right here,' he said.

'Where?' I asked, confused. I couldn't see anything.

Suddenly there was a scream, a cry of rage and insanity, and the sound of crashing and smashing of tea cups and whatnot. Then other voices joined in, shouting, wailing and moaning. Orderlies and nurses and doctors tried to yell above the rising noise as four men hauled away the same big Frankenstein who had grabbed the woman's breasts on the day I arrived. Since then he had been sedated and straightjacketed, and this was his first outing back on planet earth, but it wasn't going too well. Poor man.

The whole herd was catching the freak-out, doing the heebie-jeebie zombie dance, and the rest of the staff quickly gathered them and marshalled them back into the main building and to their dormitories. The screaming continued in the distance as the yard cleared and everyone filed up the stairs. We were left standing behind the little hut.

Then Nutso says, 'Now is a good time to go.'

No fucking kidding, Nutso.

It was almost noon, the middle of the day, and he knelt down at the fence and deftly undid the wire till there was a hole big enough to crawl through.

'Now?' I was totally unprepared. It was so sudden, like when you were a kid and everyone was on the roundabout in the park, going faster and faster with only one spot open, and if you missed it you fell on your face.

'Now we just walk down the hill to that building over there and we visit my girlfriend.' He grinned a manic grin and crawled through the hole.

'Girlfriend?'

I crawled after him, thinking of my beautiful velvet suit that I'd left behind. You don't just crawl through the hole. That is just the result, the culmination of so much focus. Like a swan dive at the Olympics. My head goes through and I know right there that my intentions are clear now and, if I'm caught again, my unblemished slate at Sterkfontein will have the words 'escape risk' scrawled across it. The doctors will possibly guess that I set the whole thing up just for this purpose. Halfway through I am thinking … Is this it? Is this the time? Should I go back? There is still time. What about my suit, my beautiful suit? Oh fuck. Jesus, Allah, Elvis, Chunkie Charlie, I need you!

Once I was through the hole, on the other side, Nutso carefully wove the strands back together again. On the outside looking in. Nobody had come out of the building looking for us yet.

'Nice job,' I murmured as he finished up his work.

'Keep them guessing,' he chuckled with a mischievous grin.

We strolled casually across the veld like we belonged there and made our way down the gentle slope to the bottom of the valley to the large institutional building with no fence. We walked up the stairs and into the hallway. A young woman came out of a room and stared at us.

'Hi,' she said tentatively, almost conspiratorially. 'What are you doing here?'

'Oh, we've just come to visit Marie.'

She became agitated, looking this way and that.

'No, this is not visiting time. You must go.' She pushed the air in front of her with both hands. 'You got to go.'

'Okay, okay, we'll go, but you tell her I was here to see her.'

'Ja, but …'

'Don't tell anyone else!'

We carried on walking down the long corridor to another exit. The woman was still watching us as the door closed and we headed down the stairs, away from the place and up the long hill. Or was it a mountain?

ON THE RUN

On the run is a state of mind. Harried and hurried and busy, busy, busy. We walked. We were still too close. We couldn't run yet, so we casually strolled as if this was something we did every day. We walked in full view of all the compounds in the distance as if we were *trustees*, but we were escaping. Further and further. We walked away from the madness and up the hill, faster and faster. It seemed to go on forever. I didn't want to turn around. Up the slope we walked until we heard a shout in the distance, just caught on a breeze and lifted in the air. Then we started running.

A kilometre and a half behind us, figures emerged from the compound. Coming for us were two men in white coats accompanied by two trustees and, straining hard on their leashes and barking, two very excited bloodhounds. Now we could hear the baying of the dogs. How did this happen? How did my life turn out this way? I remember James Cagney running to the lighthouse, barefoot in the fog, the sound of bloodhounds signalling his doom.

You'll never take me alive, copper.

We were near the top of the hill. Running. Running up the steep incline. Dogs. Men in white coats and half-crazy guys, *trustees*, trying to earn points by demonstrating their sanity, their social responsibility, those medicated deputies drooling from the corners of their mouths, lumbering as only the drugged, the somnolescent, can. This is a movie. This is my life. How did it happen? (Did I take the brown acid?) How did I fall into this nightmare? I am now crossing the border into legend, becoming the words in an epic poem, falling from reality, trapped in the chorus of a pop song.

'Quick Joey Small (Run Joey Run)'. A goddamn bubblegum song.

'Look everybody, I am still here – it's me! Can you see me? I am the same old me.'

I have had nightmares like this. When I was locked up drinking brandy in the frozen winter cell I only dreamed of the possibility, to be there in the open with a chance, just one slim chance, but decades later I still had nightmares like this. Running, running, running. Sometimes you've got to be careful what you wish for ...

This was a pivotal moment in real life. You make your move, decisively and confidently. And you run, chest pounding, heart breaking and air rushing over your cheekbones. There is no stopping, no getting depressed. No feeling bad. No stitches. No 'not in the mood'. You just run. Run. Run. These are the Olympics of Life. There is no glory, no endorsement; there is just the knowledge that NOW is the time to make your break.

My father was a runner. After he left, he became a vegetarian or a vegan or something, and he became a long-distance runner, finishing in the top five at the 100-mile marathon held at Green Point Stadium. He ran from us to search for himself. Did he succeed? I will never know. I never saw him again.

As a consequence of his healthy eating and athletic endeavours I took up cigarette smoking and spurned all sporting activity except hockey, because the school forced us to play a sport. Yet here I was. Running. Not like an amateur, competing for self-worth and feeling good about my effort. No. I was running in real life. I was doing the very thing that all these sporting events are based on. I was running from the predator. Fleeing for my life. There was no room for second place, no runner-up medal. Just win or lose.

You reach deep and quickly feel your lungs, gasping, like a fish tossed on the dock early in the morning, dry ice smoking. All you are is the pain in the chest. I want to swim. I want to swim. I want to dive in water and arc so smoothly, instead of running up on land, where it hurts so. This is unnatural, painful. I want to go back, back to the time when we were one, the water smooth and close as we all turned together, dancing in the stream of time. But I can't, I am stuck on this dry land so far from the ocean, so I run in a dream.

And run, if you will, to the top of the hill.

My shoes were ruined, my nice white takkies meant for cruising on the boulevard.

When I finally reached the top of the rise I turned around. They were still more than a kilometre behind us. If they just let those dogs go they would have us, but this was a hospital, not a prison. In The Fort the legend was that the guards at Pretoria Central had horses that they rode while the prisoners were working in the fields, and the horses were trained to bite. I kept having visions of men on horseback hunting down unarmed prey, the giant-jawed horses lunging with bloodstained teeth and frothy drool. I ran faster.

They were going up and we were going down. Now we really pumped it, flying over rocks and anthills. *Run Erich run!* Faster, faster, faster, till we got to the bottom. Ahead of us was a farm and trees, lots of trees, and we disappeared under their cover before our pursuers crested the hill. We ran in the shade on an old gravel road that skirted the farm, but I was tired.

I couldn't keep it up. For months I had been sitting indoors smoking cigarettes and living on crap for food. It looked like the land was becoming treeless again and we would be running in the open, totally exposed and easy to corner. There was probably already a vehicle dispatched along the roads coming from the other side to trap us in a pincer movement. We were not the first to run and there must have been some standard contingency plans for these predictable routes.

I had heard that the trustees were allowed to 'teach a lesson' to anyone who made a break for it. Accidents can happen when you run crazy in the bush. We could hear the dogs at the top of the hill baying. Not barking, but baying. A sinister sound: *'Aroo, aroo, aroo.'* Thankfully not growling and gnashing like a police German shepherd, all teeth and long snout. But baying? I thought they just made that up for books and movies, like those old American black-and-white films about chain gangs in the Southern states, but there it was, like some drunken love-struck wolf warning us that it was coming. There is definitely no subtlety about the old bloodhound on your trail.

The noise had attracted the dogs from the farm and they were all lining the fence like a welcoming committee, tails wagging, answering their doggie pals.

I went off the road behind a tree to find a hiding place, thinking I could maybe lie down behind a bush and curl into a ball and hope for the best when they started kicking me. Instead I lost my footing and fell through a covering of dry branches, like a Tarzan trap, and into an old dry drainage ditch which was probably filled with water in the rainy times. I looked inside and could see nothing but a dark tunnel which I imagined was filled with snakes and spiders. The perfect hiding place.

Nutso saw me fall and wanted to jump in with me, but I sent him further down the ditch so only one of us could get caught at a time. I watched him disappear into the ground and then I crawled towards the darkness that crackled and rustled with all kinds of tiny noises.

Out on the road the barking became more furious and it seemed that the farm dogs were causing a problem for the hunters, distracting the bloodhounds from their job just at the point where we had veered off the gravel road. I lay perfectly still as people shouted at the dogs, which didn't listen, and then I heard the sound of vehicles. I was praying. I am not sure to whom, just a generalised plea to any spirits that might be lurking in the area, but I was praying.

Or maybe it was gambling, you know, when you spin the wheel and the little ball flies round and round and you have your rent money on the table and you close your eyes, clench your hands, people all around stop breathing, and you hear the sound of the prayer. 'Please, please, please let it be my turn.'

Please, please, please don't let there be any witnesses, some little boy out with cattle, a farmer smoking his pipe, somebody exceedingly helpful to say that they are there, there by the tree. Please, please don't let the dogs smell me or the people kick me, or scorpions and snakes bite me so I pass out and die and then float out with the next rains.

I lay there for hours. Numb. The din subsided and the people and dogs withdrew. I slept and dreamed. It reminded me of when I used to play truant, hiding in the bushes, trying to trap mice. Now I was the mouse. Finally, after hours and hours, I just had to get up. Perhaps we should have waited for nightfall, but there was so much eerie rustling in the bushes and I was finished with that. I popped up out of the earth and saw Nutso lying under a tree. It was quiet.

The bush thrummed with crickets like a calm Sunday afternoon.

Rebirth. Am I reborn or am I simply in some kind of limbo? I seem to be alive and the four walls no longer surround me.

Now that I was out of the prison, now that I was out of the madhouse, now, the common wisdom would exclaim, I was even deeper in trouble than before. I suppose, in the classical sense, I was. I was especially in danger of some serious physical discipline by government thugs. I had not yet been sentenced, and that was a good thing, because escaping from prison while sentenced earned huge amounts of time on top of the existing sentence. To a prison warder, escape is worse than murder. But I'd escaped from a nuthouse, a mad action by a crazy man.

Yet I was free. Wasn't I? I mean, what is freedom? Before they put me in jail I had freedom of movement. Black people had to carry pass books and needed permission to go from one place to another. Maybe I was like that now. But I could move. I had taken back what was stolen from me. It was a powerful victory.

Free again to move, I who lived in motion, always restless, always on the move, movement itself being a therapy, a thinking aid. Since I was seventeen I had been moving. To lock me, to cage me like a monkey, a lion ... to clip my wings so that I could never again fly on the wind ... that's what they wanted.

Kill me first.

But already something had happened. While I'd been locked away, it was terrible, depressingly claustrophobic, but inside, when the worst was going down, when all was lost ... something had changed within me. I had become almost brave. It was a revelation, to see that when all was lost I had untapped resources. When I was powerless and shocked, the joker came to the surface. The gallows jester.

Now that I was out, something had happened to me. Already in my freedom my courage seemed to be slipping away. The secret agent that lived inside my brain, the madcap laugher that strutted with flamboyant pride through the night-time corridors of John Vorster Square, he had already gone. He didn't like this part of the play.

Who was that unmasked man? Where did he come from? Why doesn't he stay? I see him galloping away, waving adieu and shouting, 'See you again – next time you die,' and I feel empty. No, not empty, just human and frail. I am in the world of the living and I am afraid. I feel it, the fear, the cold hand of fear that this new life will be taken away.

My courage is gone now that I am free. All I have left is cold determination. Now I am again a small human being with something precious to lose. Even that makes me feel like such a coward. Will I always live in fear from now on? No more Mr Casual, no devil-may-care, no more contemptuous prince of the highway armed with the superiority of youth.

I am worried. This is what I have become. Fearful and worried. Suspicious and cynical. I don't have time yet to mourn for the death of me, just another casualty in the running battle, another unnamed victim in the fickle war of life, some piece of me left behind in one of those dirty places. I was so brave when everything was lost. What would I become now that I had regained my living body? I was afraid. I felt so small and humbled.

And I was already planning to get rid of Nutso at the first opportunity.

24

AFTER I ESCAPED

Running free over the veld. (At this juncture we switch to slo-mo cam. Blond hair flying, pull up the title song from the soundtrack and milk the emotional moment.)

Nutso and me. We walked along the country road, the gravel of the Transvaal on our shoes, as it had been for so many in my family before me, and we sang a song written by an American, because we had no songs of our own, something like ...

Well, I've got to run to keep from hiding
And I'm bound to keep on riding
And I've got one more silver dollar
But I'm not gonna let 'em catch me, no
Not gonna let 'em catch the midnight rider

Allman Brothers. Fucking pop culture fills all the cracks in our faithless lives.

And then we got to a road and found a phone. I was able to get an operator and made a reverse-charge call to my mother. I didn't want to worry her, but I needed to get Carl's phone number, because he lived in Pretoria, where we seemed to be headed. She had been in contact with Carl's mother while we were sharing our cell in John Vorster Square. I had no idea where Carl was, whether he was still locked up in another prison or if he had been released on bail, or how he would react to hearing from me, trouble on the move. Also, I was still unsure whether he was just a nice guy or an exceptionally devious undercover policeman using me as a foil to gain credibility in the criminal underworld, but I knew that we had made some genuine connection. At that stage he was one of the few cards in my tattered pack, and all I could do was gamble and hope for the best. Without a helping hand from him, even just a ride back to Johannesburg to Bridget's lair, I was marooned on foot and easy to spot.

I was lucky to catch my mother at home. While it was good to hear her voice I was filled with regret at being such a burden, bringing nothing but sadness and worry.

'Hi, how are you?' I began with the standard ice-breaker.

'I'm okay, we are doing well,' she answered. 'But what about you, are you all right? Are conditions better where you are?'

'Well, that's just the thing … I'm not actually there any more,' I offered.

'What? They've moved you somewhere else?'

'No, no, not exactly,' I replied cagily. 'I saw a window of opportunity and I took it, you know, and now I am just looking for Carl's phone number.'

'Oh. Ooooh. Oh shit!' she exclaimed. 'Oh my god, why? What are you going to do?'

'I can't say, I don't know … but it is done, Shirley. I just need Carl's number.'

'Just wait a moment, I have it here.' She gave me the number, and then she said, 'Remember, Erich, we love you.'

'And I love you too. I must go now. Bye.'

'Bye and stay safe,' she wished against all odds.

Nutso and I stood at the side of the road and stuck out our thumbs, and damned if the first car that came by, a Mercedes-Benz driven by a grey-haired farmer, didn't just pull off and wait for us to come running. We were respectful, calling him *Oom* and all, making like Happy White People, and so I began my new life of lying to stay alive, a life of disguises and aliases and a different story for every circumstance. Nobody was trusted any more. There was a new thing happening and it was always present, this feeling, this cold knowledge that the only certainty was to trust nobody, and always expect the worst from everyone. I resolved never to show surprise even if the worst thing in the world happened and all my nightmares came true. I would never let the world see me break, even when I was crying like a baby inside.

'Thank you, Oom, ja, no, we were out there riding our scrambler, our motorbike. Man that was fun, hey?' I looked at Nutso.

'Crazy, man, crazy,' he confirmed with a light laugh and an open smile.

'But you see, sir,' I continued, 'there was this hole in the ground and then there was this tree, it wasn't there, then suddenly it jumps in front of us when we turn, and now we have to go get my oupa's bakkie and come back to get the bike.' I waited for him to pull out a gun and shoot us.

'Ag, ja, you boys look like you have been fighting with bushes. I'm going in to Pretoria – I can drop you in the city, there by the Kerk Plein, where there's telephones too, if you need to call someone.'

'Yes, sir, please, thank you very much.'

As we drove I told him that we – me and my 'cousin' – were having such fun, and that I was at university ... where I was studying hard, learning how to tell lies to nice men in German cars.

★★★★★★★★★★ **25** ★★★★★★★★★★

PRETORIA

Pretoria. The heart of the Afrikaner empire, the city where my father was born, into the tribe I never knew. This was where the army headquarters were. This was where the police were trained. The kind old gent dropped us at the main square downtown and it was like being in a war film. Every second person wore a uniform. There were soldiers and policemen everywhere.

I dialled Carl's number from a phone box and was amazed when he answered the phone himself. Surely the gods were smiling on me that day.

'Hey Carlo, howzit going? This is Erich, your old flatmate.'

'Erich! What the fuck, are you out already?'

'Ja man, but you know, they were a little slow on the uptake, so I had to make my own move, if you know what I mean.'

'You mean ... a self-release programme?' He burst into laughter.

'Ja, it's the only one I qualified for.'

'Where the fuck are you?'

'In Pretoria, downtown, at the corner of Kerk Street on the Church Square, and I was just wondering if you knew anybody who was going to Joburg who could give me and my friend a lift.'

'Wait right there,' he shouted excitedly. 'I'll be there in a half an hour.'

We stood there, surrounded by these people, two scruffy kids, young men freshly bust out of the nuthouse. Me with my long blond hair and my old blue jeans that had been patched over and over again, every stitch replaced and then covered with the giant marijuana plant crawling up the legs.

And then he comes, Carl in his BMW with his dog in the back seat, a yuppie ten years ahead of his time, dressed in expensive designer jeans and a warm woollen cardigan with a collar, pulling up to the pavement and opening the passenger door for me.

'Welcome back, my brother.' He looked happy to see me. Nutso hopped in the back seat.

'I've got something for you, for all the times you shared with me,' Carl said, and he handed me a bag with not one, but two barbecue chickens, hot and steaming, the smell of it – the sweet dreams of youth.

'Thanks, man, thanks.'

Then he reached behind his seat and retrieved another bag which he gave to me, a bottle of Jack Daniel's, and then he reached under the seat and gave me one more thing – a roll, twenty sticks of Durban Poison – and we drove out into the hills beyond Pretoria and parked high and secluded on a gravel hillock under a row of tall bluegum trees, where we ate and drank and smoked and talked about what had happened to each of us since we left John Vorster Square. His mother had arranged it all for him with money and influence, he told me.

Bless the mothers of this world.

Once we were well on our way to feeling good, Carl, as hypnotically persuasive as ever, convinced Nutso that he needed to be dropped off on the highway so he could make his way to Joburg. He was a bit of a liability to have around, because he really did belong in some kind of care. I certainly couldn't be seen wandering around with him. He had that naivety that only the mentally unbalanced have, but also he was a ticking bomb. I didn't know if, or when, he would have some attack, some mania, and go on a freak-out rampage without his medication.

We were not friends. Not partners. He was crazy. He knew it and liked it. I had used him and now I needed to dump him. Any police alert would be for two guys, so I needed to be one again. And I had plans. They hadn't changed. The plan was to leave the country. It got a bit vague after that. I would go and live happily ever after in London, where they all hated apartheid, and I would play music and study literature and psychology, or else maybe I would go to Russia and become a communist.

That seemed a little bleak, though. Western propaganda didn't paint a rosy picture of life inside the Soviet republics. In fact, aside from the capitalist versus communist difference, it seemed to be about the same as home. Secret police, traitors and violence. A life of shit.

Anyway, I think Nutso was just looking for a little jol on the town before being sent back to the cage. I had no intention of going back. *You'll never take me alive, copper.* Depression, anger and fear combined make a dangerous animal.

Then we went to Carl's *pozi* somewhere there in the Pretoria suburbs. I was too far gone to remember anything, just a blur of details, plus I needed to sleep. I had just run over a mountain, chased by dogs, white coats and madmen, and I had cowered in ditches, but Carl insisted on fitting me out in an Armani suit and possibly gave me some drug, LSD maybe, and we were out in some club and then there was vomiting involved and I woke up with just the vaguest recollection. I have no idea what happened. Not too smart.

The next morning I got Carl to drive me to Johannesburg and drop me a few blocks away from Endicott's house in Parktown where the shit had gone down, and I said goodbye to the smooth-talking Afrikaner prince and moved into the unknown. When the nights were dark and the wind blew cold it had been me and him stranded in a hostile environment, castaways in a concrete ocean, and for a while we had shared everything like brothers, and we had survived. Now he had harboured and helped me as a fugitive. But still ...

I didn't trust Carl, no offence intended. I couldn't. It was the cold, calculating and necessary headspace of survival. Trust nobody and hope for the best. I was like a homing pigeon. I didn't know where to go, so like all criminals I was being drawn back to the scene of the crime. As soon as Carl was gone I doubled back and ran down the road to Skinny Girl's house, to someone who was not involved in anything criminal and didn't do drugs. I needed a neutral base to contact Bridget, whose number was on a piece of paper in my pocket.

Skinny Girl was a strange chick with an eating disorder that kept her perilously close to death, but we had a friendship of sorts. She was associated with Endicott's crew and with the Durban bunch in the house round the corner and up the hill. I was as predictable as any fugitive. There I was, six blocks from the only house I really knew in Joburg. I phoned Bridget at her flat in the Bronx.

'Hey, Bridget baby, how's it rocking on your end?' I began, but was quickly drowned out. She was supremely pissed off.

'What the hell do you think you are doing?' she screamed, and I had to hold the phone away from my ear as she yelled her tale to me.

About an hour after I'd escaped through the wire, they had all come to visit me at Sterkfontein in Endicott's VW van with bottles of wine and all kinds of tasty things for me. Bridget had finally put some money down and got me a real living, breathing lawyer. 'Now you've really gone and blown it,' she said. She told me that Boetman and a squad of policemen had been to Endicott's house already and that they were quite friendly, *not at all angry*.

'Endicott says they told him to tell you to *just give yourself up and there will be no repercussions*.'

Endicott. My good old friend, my band-mate, my late-night confidant. We had some good times together, in the old days in Cape Town. He had an old Bridgestone motorbike and we used to go home with the sun rising, doing the run from Long Street out to Milnerton, the wind so strong that we would do the whole route at a forty-five-degree angle to stop being blown away. Scared, breathless, laughing. But something had happened. I wasn't sure about my friend any more.

'Bridget, thank you for everything, but I can't go back. In this law, this court, this country, I am guilty, and there is no way a lawyer can get me off. I don't trust them, the police, the lawyers ... even my friends. I have no bribes for the judge and if I surrender I am going to have my teeth kicked out and my ribs broken. If I keep playing the mad thing they can do stuff to me with machines and drugs. If I get certified I'll be there till I die maybe.'

'So you gonna run?' she finally asked in a quiet voice.

'So I'm gonna run. I'm going to stay free till they catch me.'

'Fucking idiot – you'll never make it, but I will help you.'

It was strange, but, of all people, I trusted her to be true to her word. The Mathematics flowed strong in her veins.

★★★★★★★★★★ **26** ★★★★★★★★★★

WHILE I WAS SLEEPING

After I hung up the phone, Skinny Girl told me the strangest thing. She said that the 'maid' Gladys at Endicott's house had told her that Samson was the one who covered me in wood the night before I was arrested. At first it didn't penetrate my brain. *Samson covered me in wood?*

'Yes,' she said, 'he covered you in wood *so the police wouldn't see you.*'

That means the police had already been there the night before, looking for me, as I lay passed out in the garage. I knew that Skinny Girl was telling the truth. Everybody knew about her deep, sisterly relationship with Gladys and sometimes commented on the inappropriateness of it by putting it down to her tenuous mental state.

'Ja, well, she's fucken cuckoo,' was the consensus.

Perhaps it was because I grew up so poor and that in our household we didn't have any hired help, no 'maids' or gardeners, that I was free of the standard programming. Anyway, old Samson and I got along just fine, and, while everyone else was out doing their nine-to-five, we would sit out in the backyard on peach boxes drinking tea or beer and talking away as he told me about life in Soweto.

In the many identities of my youth, I related strongly to the Kullid people of Cape Town because of their beautiful language and the fact that we shared the same city, and I was Jewish by osmosis, from being among lovely liberal Jewish kids in my school, but the strongest at the time was my English identity. So strong was it that I never once thought of myself as a Boer, or as African. My mother's tongue was English, and her mother had been brought to South Africa as a new bride from the Isle of Jersey in 1919, after the Great War.

My South African–born 'English' grandfather had fought at Delville Wood in France, along with his brother who perished there, and the returning hero brought home his trophy, a pretty woman of good family, Marguerite Isabella Noel, the daughter of an architect, who had served as a nurse in the war. Tough stock for Africa!

In my head were all these hard-wired paradigms. I was English. My influences were English, Scottish, Irish and Welsh. English people were nice. They had the best sense of humour. They had fought the Evil Dog Hitler who had tried to exterminate the families of my Jewish friends. Afrikaners were racist. Afrikaners were Nazi-lovers. Afrikaners hated the Jews and they hated the English and they hated the Kullids and they hated all black Africans. So I hated the Afrikaans language and the Boer people. I hated with the ferocity of a Boer because inside me was an Unexploded Boer. I hated them because of the Kullids, the Jews, the Africans and the English. I hated them as a frontline soldier flying the freedom flag of Rock 'n' Roll.

Oh, those lovely English with their Beatles and Carnaby Street and cool cats in Afghan coats. The English in South Africa maintained an aloof presence when it came to the hard-core Boers. They joked among themselves how uncouth and how vulgar the Boers were. They languished in their transplanted English culture, drinking wine, sending children to eisteddfods and gymkhanas and making a shitload of money. Of course, the making of the money was completely thanks to the Boers, who created the economic palette with which these English could paint their golden pictures.

The English quietly supported apartheid and racism, but they didn't talk about it. They thought that the country should be 'nicer' in its application of the 'rules'. Of course the black man, the native, should *know his place*, but there was no need to be so nasty about it. So they just lived the high life and pretended that they, the nice, civilised English who were good because they beat Hitler, had nothing to do with those *verkrampte* farmers who ran the country; but secretly, when elections came, they voted for the Boer party because, stupid as they were, *those Boers certainly knew how to deal with the black problem.*

How could they do this? How could they remain in such denial? My mother told me that they wore 'blinkers' inside their brains, like horses used to wear in the city, so they couldn't see the things that scared them. Try as I might, I hardly ever got any young person to talk politics, because it was just *so uncool*, but if I did succeed in engaging someone, they would always tell me that I hadn't even been to university so I just didn't understand anything. I was stupid, uneducated.

I disagreed. They not only had blinkers; they were completely and utterly *toe*. They could not see what was in front of their eyes because they already knew the truth and the truth set them free, free from the real world. What gave them this amazing aloof power, this superior intellectualism?

English people could keep their British citizenship and they could keep it for their children too, and, as far as I knew, if you had your Brit papers you didn't have to go to the army. You didn't have to kill for the right to be superior. It was such a sweet deal. You could live the fancy life and get all the benefits of the police state, the nectar of the land could be yours to drink – all for free. No wonder they were such Happy White People.

Of course, not all English boys had that luck. Many came from families that had retreated from Rhodesia, Nigeria, Kenya, Tanzania, Zambia and other colonial paradises as they fell to independence, ruining so many cocktail parties and golf games.

These people were a little more committed to racism and muttered on about *the murderous Mau Mau who will slit your throat as you sleep*. They made their children into citizens so they could go to war, because after South Africa there were no more countries to retreat to. They would have to return to England, where they would be reduced back to their original size, their varying lowly-class and peasant statures. It was an unthinkable fate, so they decided instead to sacrifice the souls of their boys. There were no girls in the army. They were still the cheerleaders, the White Feather Women of South Africa, the militant mothers.

Before Endicott moved to Johannesburg he had lived in Cape Town and played bass guitar in the fractious, turbulent, argumentative acid-rock band Buddies, with me on drums, Deadly Hedley on guitar and El Cid on rhythm guitar and vocals as we rehearsed in The Office on Long Street, preparing for our Independent University Tour. Old Endicott got really sick with the flu just before we left, so I went over to his parents' flat where he was staying temporarily and brought a nice cold bottle of Cape see-through wine to help him get better.

Endicott's folks were very *anglais* but I never really gave much thought to where they came from, whether they were new people, come to Africa from Europe after 'the war' for a better life, or whether they were old settler stock, driven south by freedom fighters, away from the crumbling British Empire, bitter jingoist refugees retreating down the road of time. They were just niceish people; dad was lanky and distant and mom was distracted and brittle, a doily woman.

On that day, I was so up in spirits about finally going on the road with the band that I proudly mentioned to Endicott's mom that we were going to play a show at the University of the Western Cape, which was a university for brown people. Her eyes widened. Her mouth dropped. She stood still like she had seen Satan himself step through the door. Then she began screaming, this person who I thought did not speak a single word of Afrikaans.

'*Kafferboetie*! *Kafferboetie*! Filthy *kafferboetie*! Out! Out! Out of my house! Never come back, you stinking *kafferboetie*!'

She pushed me out of the door. Her face was red. Her jaws worked like she was chewing bitter poison and her neck muscles contorted in spasm as she shoved me out and slammed the door so hard that the little doily curtains fell down.

With all my cynicism, my unhappiness, my hanging in shebeens and consorting with all kinds of people of all shades, I thought I knew things. I thought I knew what was what and who was who, but that, at age eighteen or nineteen, was truly the first time I'd heard the word *kafferboetie, kaffir-brother, nigger-lover*.

It was supposed to be an insult. I rolled it around in my head. I tried it on my tongue and found that I liked it. I thought it was a title I could wear with pride. Already a lot of my Kullid friends called me *my bra*, which was a contraction of brother, *broer, broeder*, and if some older cat like Bantu Stephen Biko had come to me and said, 'Hey Little Brother of Africa, will you join with us to destroy apartheid and bring justice to this place?' I would probably have felt very proud to be his little brother, his *kafferboetie*, in that suicidal quixotic tilt.

But unfortunately, me and Stephen, we never met, and later, in 1977, the South African Police beat him to a lonely, naked, chained-up death in a prison, put there by some informers or screaming torture victims, and nobody, no dynamite-toting, Kalashnikov-wielding comrades tried to break him out. It was that kind of place, South Africa, in the year that the fat American singer, the King of Rock 'n' Roll, Elvis Presley, died on a toilet from too much money and prescription drugs.

Samson was too old to be my brother; he was more like an uncle, *'n oom*.

He couldn't pronounce the 'r' in my name, and he called me Elik when we used to sit in the back of the house on some afternoons with a couple of tall bottles of Lion Lager and a big fat zol, talking and joking. What did we talk about? What did I say that tipped the scale? One afternoon he got his girlfriend to pierce my other ear with a needle, a cork and some ice and they taught me to say a few words in Zulu.

Kunjani? Uthini?

Samson covered me in wood while I slept. Why? He found me passed out and sleeping, and they must have come for me the night before and he, Samson, covered me in wood. Why did he do it? Why did he try to help me when the game was stacked? They came the night before and Samson knew it was a bust, but he had to leave, because black men weren't allowed to be out in the white man's city at night because of the pass laws.

Was someone supposed to tell me that the drug squad were after me? Or did Samson see the truth? Just who knew what? The maddening questions that plagued me all the way through. Who? What? Why? When? Did Endicott know? Did he know that his brother had been setting me up? They were there the night before. Fuck! Samson knew that the police were there to get me and he protected me. How did he know? Were guns in evidence or was it all undercover and cool-daddy style?

It is possible that he encountered the perimeter police, the ones that they leave outside and in the street to catch or shoot anyone fleeing from the operation, and figured it all out in a flash. At least I know for sure, with no doubt, what one man did. At last I had an answer.

Samson, a man, tried to save me.

How long I slept I don't know, and just when Samson discovered me I also don't know, but he was there when the police arrived, ready to take me. He became aware of what was going on right away and knew what danger I was in. Right in front of the police he went into his 'stupid black man' act as if he was working in the yard, moving a pile of lumber from one place to another.

What he was actually doing was laying the planks carefully over me so as not to wake me up, but completely concealing me, making me the 'whitey in the woodpile'. After that he must have melted away, because it was never too smart for a black dude to be caught in white areas after dark.

While I was dead to the world, Endicott's brother arrived, bringing his friends who turned out not to be friends but the boere, the police, the *mapuza*, the stinking SAP. No matter where they looked they couldn't find me. The trap had failed and they took off for easier pickings. In the morning I woke up covered in wood and couldn't figure out what had happened. When I went into the house, Endicott kept his mouth shut. Nobody told me a thing. They were all afraid.

To this day I cannot tell who was an informer and who was not, and it really isn't important. What I remember is Samson, the black man who tried his best to save the stupid white kid from his conflicted friends. What a guy. What a true gem of a human being. The police could have killed him and nobody would have raised an eyebrow, yet he risked his life for me.

Needless to say, Endicott's brother turned up again the following morning and next thing you know some fat pig is sticking a Magnum-loaded Smith & Wesson in my hung-over face and daring me to run while his little wannabe Nazi sidekick is pointing a Parabellum with dum-dum bullets at me. I felt like a dum-dum myself.

Well, I followed Boetman's instructions and I ran, but I preferred to do it when his stupid oversized gun was not pointed at my head, which rhymes with dead.

HEROES

When I was twelve years old and my father left, something in me died, and when, a few months later, the paedophile men started reaching for my groin, the positive image of men died forever in my mind. I rejected manhood and machismo. I laughed at power tools and rugby and I endlessly taunted sportsmen, running around with their little balls and showering together, and I wore eye liner and earrings and satin shirts in the middle of the day just to freak people out. From the age of twelve to twenty there were many other small deaths in the natural decay of innocence; but that morning, the day my life ended in Johannesburg, almost put an end to the tiny part, the one per cent, the just-in-case package of me that still lived in the world of hope.

If not for Samson and his selfless act, small as it was, I could have become a true and permanent hater, but he offered me some possibility that there was something different on the planet. I spat on my generation, I pissed on whitey, but I was uplifted at the same time.

In my life it was the total breakdown of family bonding that led me to that place. My grandfathers had deserted me. They created children and deserted them and left me without history, without a story of my own, in a predatory immigrant culture. If they had something to be proud of, wouldn't they have tried to pass it on? Was it the country, the imposition of colonialism on Africa, the gruelling soul torture of living a lie every day?

I was truly a lost soul and believed that families were nothing but a false promise. What made them so empty? Why didn't they come and break me out of John Vorster Square? Was everybody in the country without honour, without romance? Even Endicott, even if fucking Endicott had set me up in some way, as it would seem at first glance – at least he did it for his brother, his older brother, his family memories, loyalties and blood. Think of it, what a terrible night of rationalisation he must have had, knowing that he wasn't going to tell me, knowing that he was going to let his friend sink for his brother's sake – unless his brother was fooling him too, brother to brother, the ancient ultimate deception.

Where was my brother, my father, my uncle? They were all gone and I was alone, sinking into the quicksand while everyone else turned their backs and made arrangements to go out for dinner. I realise now that I made some huge errors of judgement. I regarded the mission I was on not as a purely criminal black-market venture in which I would gain profit for myself, but more as a holy road, a political activity that was set against human rights violations and abuses by a police state.

I saw the money generated by the sale of the product going directly to a poor village where people lived in old tin huts because the law of the land decreed that they must. I saw part of it financing my removal from the country, leaving one less hand to pull the trigger, one less person to murder the children as they ran in terror in the street. Criminal rationalisation? How did Endicott rationalise my situation? Did I 'bring it all on myself'?

More than anything, I had bought the youth revolution thing, all that fatuous back-patting crap from the John Lennons and the Neil Youngs, those bars of Hope Soap marketed as ideals all over the world. I believed that all the young people of the world were a concerted and united force against the evils of oppression and inequality. I made the mistake of believing in my own religion.

My white friends, I realised, did not think in these terms at all, and probably considered me completely deluded. I can take wry retrospective solace, though, in the fact that, while I was wandering down the back alleys of logic, they really were the ones living in a fast-fading dream.

I wondered whether it was a national trait. Were all the young people of my generation chicken-shit people with no ... no guts, no brains, or was I just a fool, a deluded coward with flawed logic? My head spun round and round. Maybe they were just seduced by happiness, materialism and a full belly. Happiness can blind so easily; a full belly and a few beers and who cares about shit on the other side of town?

If it weren't for Samson I might have gone over the edge much further than I already was. If not for Samson I may have drowned in a leap tide of hate.

Samson tried to save me. He tried to protect me from the government men with the guns. He tried to protect me from my own friends. It's the why of it that gets me, the damn why of it all that sometimes makes me smile. His actions could have brought dire consequences, but we had been friends, or acquaintances of a sort.

Perhaps no *whitey* had ever been normal with him before, or perhaps there had been a time when they had ... and he missed it. He was old enough to remember when things had seemed to be going forward – in the fifties, when the freedom thinkers got together at the Congress of the People in Kliptown when I was only one year old and drafted the Freedom Charter ('We, the People of South Africa ...'). Perhaps someone had helped him before and he was returning the favour. Pay it forward.

The Mathematics of Honesty.

It didn't seem strange that we became such fast friends, because I'd travelled the country on my own, meeting people in strange situations, relating as only the young can. Maybe it was my naivety or my innocence that endeared me to him, or maybe he was dismayed and angered by seeing what was being done to me. Maybe we were just

Africans trying to be human. Perhaps Samson was just a normal person in the unnatural twisted apartheid world. Normal people don't desert their family and their friends. Samson simply did what any decent man would do.

The knowledge of what he did, once revealed to me, was like a breath of wind that blew on the drapes in my dark world view, and I saw something, just a glimmer, *'n glim van 'n lag*. Perhaps there really were decent men.

I don't even know his family name or whether he is still alive, but Samson will always be a part of my myth, part of my family history.

Bridget was True to Her Word and I made my way down to the suite of offices she rented in the city and hid out there for a while, and at her flat in Hillbrow. Things were very hot, as in potato, the potato being me, the situation being what it was, with informers and opportunists all over the place. Bridget had all kinds of deals going on, a new macho gangster boyfriend, and many hot pans in the fires of conspiracy. I was in the way and I was trouble: having an escapee on the grounds is just bad for biz. She quickly arranged for me to have my distinctive hair dyed brown and made kind of curly in a perm, all done in the back room of her massage parlour, where a stream of beautiful young white and brown women paraded through.

The smells of girls with their perfume and lipstick, the talcum powders, the Oil of Olay, the hair products and the nail polish. All those foreign chemicals smelled so beautiful to me, so unlike the odour of hospitals and prisons with their strong cleaning chemicals and the eternal smell of caged animals living on tobacco and producing sweat and wasted time.

Bridget went out and bought me a fabulous silver suit, a sixties piece with skinny stovepipe pants and a three-button jacket like the detectives wore, as well as a pair of glasses with regular glass in the lenses. I felt a little like the character Angel in *The Rockford Files*. ('Hey, how'd I look, Jimmy buddy? I look okay, hey, I look okay?'

And Rockford would always answer with exasperated boredom, 'Yeah, Angel, sure thing, you look just fine. Nobody will suspect that you are a no-good piece of trash, two-bit thief and con artist.') I retrieved my white leather suitcase from Derek the Taxi Driver, along with my passport, which unfortunately had expired and was useless to me. On the run with an expired passport, but, look on the bright side, boyo – I was on the run, which was a lot better than waiting for the judge to book me a room at the ever-popular Bumfuck Hotel.

Bridget was still really pissed off with me, angry because I had fucked up everything with the lawyer by escaping, ruining the plans she had concocted to bribe and bully me out of the system with legal and quasi-legal means – and you know, between you and me, I think she could have done it. Out there in heaven right now there is some judge happily enjoying eternity and thanking me for going far away. I can't begin to imagine what kind of havoc Bridget and the Pussy Posse could have wrought once they got into the judges' chambers.

She was probably also angry because she hadn't added me to her tally of men, and especially angry because I combed out the perm before it was dry and my hair frizzed out so badly that we had to cut almost all of it off and I was left with this weird short brownish-orange hair.

On a rainy winter's day in Hillbrow, sometime in July 1975, she put me in a taxi with a ticket to Cape Town and I headed for the airport. The last time I saw her, I twisted around to look through the back window of the taxi and she looked so much like that teenager from Milnerton, deceptively vulnerable, the belted raincoat, a French cigarette commercial, a diminutive figure in the rain tapping her foot angrily, impatiently, my friend Bridget.

You should take care of the treasures that you find.

Oh we can be heroes, just for one day

HOMECOMING

Landing at D.F. Malan Airport in Cape Town, out on the other side of the shantytowns, a public institution of departure and arrival, named after, dedicated to, the Boer politician who formulated the idea of apartheid, the 'visionary' leader who won the country back from the English with his dreams of Separate Development, the Art of Being Apart, who led them down the dirty road of legalised racism.

Daniel François Malan, his National Party wreaking revenge on the traitorous English-lover, the *hensopper* Jan Smuts who led the country after the Anglo-Boer War, who in 1914 bombed his Afrikaner brethren in Fietas, Fordsburg, the white ghetto of Johannesburg when the hungry Boer workers marched in solidarity with communists against the colonial *rooineks*.

But still, old General Smuts got the big airport named after him, the one in Johannesburg, while Doctor Malan ended up with the stinky little airport in Cape Town. Poor old Malan. Daniel is my second name and my Afrikaner grandfather's second name; it was a very popular name in South Africa at the time. That is almost all I knew about my grandfather, my Boer connection, and I sort of knew that we were connected to that Malan clan, because my mother used to tell me about my father's Dozens of Cousins, all Malans and Rautenbachs, racing around drinking and causing shit in some small town called Patensie, almost seven hundred kilometres up the coast. That's where my grandfather's farm was, the traditional homestead of the oldest son of the oldest son, and there was someone in our family who had married old Malan or something. Somehow we were connected. Vague stories you hear when you are a child. Ghosts of knowledge.

I had all these centuries of history spread throughout the famous families of that land, but I lived in total ignorance, surrounded by immigrant friends with foreign accents, like a settler fresh off the boat. Apart from one solitary visit from my grandfather when I was small, I had never met a single uncle, aunt or cousin on my father's side, just my little divorced grandmother, Ouma Mabel, who lived in her flat in the Cape Town suburb of Rondebosch and who always made *geelrys* when we went to visit on Sundays with my mother when I was very small.

I don't know why we were never part of the greater family, whether my father rejected his father, or the other way round. It was a mystery built around vague rumours concerning events in the early fifties when everything somehow *went bad and didn't get better*, somewhere around the time my Afrikaner father married my 'English' mother just as he was finishing his architecture degree at the University of Cape Town, but on the eve of completion, my father's final thesis, the crowning glory of his education, just 'disappeared' from the library, all his work gone, and he didn't get his degree.

At the same time my grandfather suddenly cut off all money for my father's education and he had to leave university, incomplete, without his degree, and look for work with a new family on the way. Somewhere around that time my grandfather had his sudden attack of insanity and shot the nun, as the short, immaculately incomplete legend went, a story that has left me wondering all my life just exactly why a man from the farm would stalk and shoot a Bride of Christ. What devilish and demonic fantasy could have fuelled his crazy actions?

When I was five or six years old, around 1960, he came to visit us once, just after his release from his nine-year stint in Valkenberg, on the eve of Christmas. He came to our hungry, spare house in Fish Hoek, bringing so much food in a station wagon, just like a regular *nagmaal* feast, more than I had ever dreamt of. That was the only time I saw my oupa. Before that night I never knew I had one, and after that night I never forgot. He never came back again, never sent a birthday card, and left nothing when he died.

I was so close to the source, to the people who were controlling the destiny of the country, and yet so distant. Some simple twist of fate and I could have been there. *I could'a been a contender*, I could have been a Boer. I should have been a Boer, shooting terrs on the border, driving my Casspir through the townships in all my self-righteous glory, revelling in the power and the might of the Holy Right.

Belonging, being from – all the things put together that make you from some place. What are they, what is real and what is perceived? Boers had a sense of belonging. They built a culture around belonging and they bolstered and fortified their arguments with lies and omissions and mixed it all with supernatural superstitions from the Middle East and the Roman Empire (aka Christianity).

Nothing wrong with that. All countries and cultures have done that over the ages, using creation myths and fabricated nostalgias to create citizens who all believe much the same thing. Whether the Hebrews or the Haida, they all have fabulous and often savage stories that weave and entrance, that establish their people as the chosen, the favourite, the ones destined to rule, the people set apart and loved above all by the Creator.

If we didn't have this 'education' we would all believe different things and have different truths. We would be very, very unmanageable. Much of a person's 'national identity' has been manufactured into them from outside sources, from church pulpits, government-controlled media and the carefully edited history books in the education system. And we seem to be hard-wired to desire these stories, with our ingrained need to belong to a social unit. People watch sport or television and they experience the same thing at the same time, and the shared experience comforts them in the loneliness of the universe, in the scary chasm of this life, the feeling of common experience. The herd. The sheep all waiting for The Shepherd.

I was the classic mentally ill isolationist, the lone dog, breathing hot air and bravado in place of information and confidence. I believed in nothing and I mocked all the creation myths and national dreams as childish stories for fools who had willingly surrendered the ability to think for themselves. I had convinced myself to my mental core that I had nothing, absolutely nothing, invested in that demented place, South Africa, Cape Town, whatever, and I would blow away my existence like a handful of salt. Poof. Like yesterday's cocaine.

But belief is belief. Just like the fools who believed the National Bullshit Paradigm, I too had constructed my own religion, cobbled together from my own mistaken conclusions and willing self-deceptions, and I believed implicitly in what my priest, the cold, grey *dominee* of depression, told me in the depths of my despair. I followed my national leader, my great inspiration, the alienated bitterness of the *bittereinder*, leading me on to ever more hopeless thoughts. I was an exile in my own home.

Just like the Boer people, I was following strange philosophies. I was just as deluded as they were, but I had no company and that was okay, because in my religion, in my parliament, I needed only me. I was Aces Out. Solitary Man. My simple credo was fuck you, fuck you, and fuck you too.

Yes, I believed all that. In my philosophy I would walk away, head held high, and never look back, because I did not belong in that cultural, ethical, moral and artistic anachronism.

Oh, and by the way, fuck you too!

As I arrived in the city by taxi, the first thing I saw was that a piece of it was gone, a whole neighbourhood, block after block was gone, more than a neighbourhood, a borough; the living beating heart of the city had been hacked out, leaving a bright fresh orange gravel scar. They had been chipping away at it for years, but now suddenly a huge piece of District Six had completely disappeared, along with all the people. The city was still noisy, but something was missing. It had been mortally wounded. Nowadays they call it ethnic cleansing.

HOMECOMING

Who let this happen?

While I was gone, locked up in the cold north, they took all the people, *what they called the non-white, the non-European, the darkies, the Kullids, the hotnots, the savage drunken layabouts, the refuse, the eyesores, the goffels, the festering nest of crime and vice,* away from the centre of the city and moved them far, far away, and they bulldozed their houses, they removed all evidence.

Where were the people?

All that was left were the empty streets and empty lots, just dust and gravel, like nobody had ever lived there. Before the Europeans arrived at the Cape, the Khoikhoi people had been here, the so-called Hottentots, the '*hotnots*', the lowest of the low, those curly-headed *skelms* who just refused to understand who was *baas*.

The white colonists tried everything to help the First People. First they tried to give them jobs, but those wily cattle owners didn't like the idea very much of slaving away for some gin-swigging ponce in a wig, so the whites had to import slaves from other countries to do the work, a very expensive undertaking. Then they introduced the Khoi to smallpox and alcohol and topped it off with real estate, producing pieces of paper that gave them the power to steal land from them. And then, fuck it, they turned them into wage slaves anyway and, when they were naughty, put them in irons and sometimes bricked them live into the walls of the Company Castle, where they were discovered centuries later. After hours the good burghers went to the Castle and fucked into being a new breed of slaves – their own bastard children.

In my days of youth they would say to me that there were no more.

'*No man, the hotnots is all gone. There's none left. Those Kullid peoples is just descended from the Malays and Indians and Madagascar slaves. There's no natives here. The ones that was, they left – the Griquas and Namas and Basters – they all fucked off. This is God's town now. It belongs to the Christians, the Muslims and the Jews and is absolutely, definitely for sure, one hundred per cent and more, not the Homeland, not the Holy Land to some gogga-worshipping monkey* boys who wouldn't know shit from piss if you served it on a tray, no matter how long some Ikey scientist says they lived there.'

So they just kicked them out for some architectural fantasy mixed with social engineering at its lowest form. In what office up there in *Boerbefok* land did they think up these vile corruptions? Fucking B.J. Vorster!

Jou ma se fok se moer, Vorster!

Everybody was gone.

Home was bleak that winter, and the bleakness was in me too. It was cold and rainy and the wind raged across the bay. Low fogs moved mysteriously among the trees on the slopes of the mountain. It was so fabulously sombre to put on a raincoat and a hat and walk up through the trees, a shadow, a ghost on the mountain. I could disappear with all the other ghosts.

I went to see Deadly Hedley the Guitar King where he was living in an old converted office block just off Long Street, and he gave me a warm sheepskin coat and told me to come to a party with the boys that Friday.

I went down the hallway to use his communal toilet and found that there was no toilet paper, just scraps of newspaper cut into squares hanging on a hook. While I was sitting there, luxuriating in the fact that there was no cellmate to share the shitty experience with, I took the first square of newspaper off the hook and started to read the news story. It was about the death, the murder, of Sean Rafferty, the long-time scenester and party lord who was known far and wide, from Bakoven to Bonteheuwel. Gone. Found dead in that little park at the base of the cliff that used to be a quarry up under Signal Hill on Strand Street. 'Drug deal gone bad or gang revenge,' the reporter surmised. Oh Sean …?

In the late sixties and early seventies no party, no happening, would be truly under way without the irrepressible spirit and unhampered mirth and vitality of Tommy Tottenham and Sean Rafferty, a rakish pair of drunken gentlemen who talked in wide brogues and swaggered about the town with no care whatsoever for laws or skin colour or police or time of day. They were outrageous and disrespectful and one whole lot of fun and sure to come to a bad end. (You mark my words. A bad end.)

One time I saw him, Sean, in Sea Point, walking through the hurly-burly, the hustle and bustle of pedestrians, smoking a long three-blader and talking in a loud voice. All the cops knew Sean and a *polies* van was following him, a Chevrolet with a blue light on top. So he turned around and walked straight up to the vehicle, and leant up against it, depositing his joint in the little water gutter where the window joined the roof.

'Top of the morning to you, Herr Sergeant Kapitan, and how are you today?'

'You stink like dagga,' the constable said, and both cops jumped out of the vehicle, spread him up against the van, and performed a humiliating public search right there in front of everybody on Sea Point Main Road at eleven o'clock on a Saturday morning. But they found nothing.

'You watch out, Rafferty, we got our eyes on you.'

As the cops were about to drive away, Sean reached out and retrieved his zol from the roof of the Chevy *kwela-kwela*, and continued his smoky promenade through the horrified citizenry.

I wiped myself clean with the death of Sean Rafferty while trying to remember the words to an old song by Dave Davies of the Kinks, a plaintive little memorial, 'Death of a Clown'.

The old fortune teller lies dead on the floor
Nobody needs fortunes told any more
Let's all drink to the death of a clown.

I didn't go to the house party that Deadly Hedley invited me to, and I learnt the next day, when I bumped into Sexy Sylvia coming out of the booze shop on Mill Street, that the police had swooped and busted everybody for possession of this and that, and they were all locked up down in Caledon Street Police Station.

I was shocked by the arbitrary closeness of disaster. Those police – they were relentless when it came to harassing unarmed, slightly wasted young citizens. I could have been there! I could have been put back in the system just by mistake. Behind the walls again. That should have been warning enough for me to fade quietly away, but instead, on the Monday I put on my sheepskin coat and, like a total fool, went downtown to the police-infested court with my collar turned up and a big scarf half covering my face, and I sat in the back and watched as they were arraigned. Deadly Hedley was standing in the dock with Long Street Steve and the G-Man, co-accused and bedraggled, in the same clothes they had been wearing for days.

ROYAL FLUSH

It was a quick court appearance for Deadly Hedley and Steve, the judge looking at them with disdain, shaking his head as he read the charges, and remanding them back into custody till their trial, but also granting a reasonable bail of thirty rand if they could make it.

As they were led from the court, I left my seat and made one more stupid decision. I approached the bailiff and asked if it was possible to visit one of the prisoners, and I was directed to a policeman sitting at a desk. After telling him that I wished to see Deadly Hedley, he took me backstage to the holding cells, behind barred doors. This court was a rinky-dink little affair, nothing like the grand caverns in Johannesburg, but the smell was there, old tobacco and sweat. I was in a prison and I didn't like it at all. I sat there in the small visiting room till they brought the Guitar King to me.

He entered the room, his long blond hair half covering his hawk-like face and he stared in surprise, and then looked around conspiratorially to see if anyone was listening.

'What the fuck are you doing here, brother?' he hissed in a loud whisper.

'I dunno,' I shrugged my shoulders. 'I came to see if I could do anything, bring you cats some smokes.' I tossed him my almost full pack of Texans.

'Shit, thanks buddy, you got any matches?' he asked, and then added, 'Maybe you could go to my parents and see if they will bail me out.' This was a first for me. Even though Deadly Hedley had been to my mother's house, had many animated conversations and cups of tea with her, and even dated my little sister when she was old enough, being the insatiable rake that he was, I had never met his family. He gave me their address and a little advice.

'It's good to see you,' he said, 'but don't come back, you fool. Stay away from the police.'

I left the boys in the court cells and I walked through the rain to his parents' address, which was quite close, a tiny, ancient single-storey house with peeling paint on Maynard Street, almost in the heart of the city. I knocked on the door and his mother answered, ushering me down the passageway to the sparse kitchen where his father sat drinking tea. They were a tall, gaunt pair, like dustbowl farmers who had lived an honest hard life and received nothing but drought and difficulties in return. When I explained to them why I was there the father exploded.

'No! No! He is nothing but trouble and he can deal with this on his own. You tell him that we will do nothing. You tell him that!'

I said I was sorry to bother them. That's all I could say to that barrage of anger that concealed deep disappointment.

There was nothing more that I could do for the Deadly One. I was suddenly feeling stupid and vulnerable walking around down in that part of town, so close to the main police station. Even if I stayed bundled up in my coat, there were a few people I had gone to school with who were actually working for the drug squad. The last thing I needed was to be seen in the neighbourhood just by chance. I couldn't help my friends so I went off to try to help myself.

I thought about Steve. I'd known him even longer than Deadly Hedley. I remember seeing him in his green school blazer in the old days at Cape Town High, him and his gang of jolly miscreants with their healthy pink cheeks, all trying to be casual, heavy and hip at the same time. Innocent. To me, even when they were bad they were innocent. And now, Steve had stood there, in the dock, like some piece of rubbish, a thief, a rapist, a con man, an embezzler, but he wasn't, he was the darling child of the Lucky City, but some people, they would make a criminal of everybody in the end, just because they could.

Me, I was rebel rubbish. I didn't have a job and I'd knowingly taken advantage of the black-market situation to dodge the government and evade the military, but not Steve. All he did was go to work five days a week, every week, and he paid his rent and then spent every single remaining cent single-mindedly getting wasted on alcohol, sending all his meagre earnings back to businesses and tax men. He had done his military service, gone to the border to kill for them, but that wasn't good enough. They still had to fuck him over.

I always felt I had let Steve down, or rather I felt that I had been given a challenge that I couldn't meet, and so it was maybe me that felt let down. The very first actual conversation with him – you know, the way you get your first impression, and it is perhaps the truest one – he talked to me and I felt in him this great hunger, this need, for guidance. It was after he had been hanging with us up at The Office, painting this giant mural on the wall. He had aspirations towards art and music in those days.

At that age he was shy, but already brave. He was humble, open and honest. These were the qualities that attracted me to him and the young friends he surrounded himself with. I had always known people my age and older. I had never looked back at the younger kids, except as 'annoyances', but these guys were so open and friendly, you couldn't help liking them. In that way he and his friends moved from their neighbourhood and school connections and into the larger community.

We were walking down Long Street talking and he stopped and looked me directly in the eye and told me how much he admired me, which was, frankly, quite embarrassing at first, the unqualified hero worship, and doubly so because I did not feel very admirable.

'I think you are so cool,' he said, 'and I would like to be like you.'

This is what I mean about him being brave. I would never ever have revealed myself that way to anybody. For a moment I thought it was a gay situation coming on, but I quickly clicked that this was something totally different; it was a kind of male-to-male communication on a level of honesty that was alien to me. His eyes shone with a total lack of subterfuge.

I suppose it may have seemed that way to him, seeing me from a distance always, a guy from the local neighbourhood, from the local school, with my pictures in the paper and in the cinemas, playing at rock festivals and the young girls going ooh and aah. I was very good at looking cool, but the drumming was not by accident alone, because it took me many years and thousands of hours of daily practice before I could kick the beat sideways.

'Tell me ... what do I do?' he asked. 'How can I get it together, how can I be cool?'

I might have been projecting myself onto him, but I felt the great yawning chasm in his being, right there as his last childish thoughts crashed upon the shores of manhood. I knew what he wanted. He wanted The Answer, The Rulebook. He wanted to know how to be. I don't know what he thought – but he came to me thinking that I must have the answer because I had it made in the world of cool.

Me, full of subterfuge, self-deception and constant thoughts of suicide, I knew exactly what he was looking for because it was the same thing I was looking for. In my mind projection he needed a father, a grandfather, and all the uncles of his village. He needed a long line of male role models to learn from, reject and rebel against and, ultimately, thank. I was the last person in the world who could fill that position, and poor Steve, it seemed that he had no village. He was simply a Child of the Lucky City.

Boys without fathers have a hole at the centre, like a school without teachers, and we are always looking, appraising, finding people who could staff our empty and deserted schools. We want to know how to do it properly. He wanted to know how to do it properly. We all do, fatherless or not. We desperately seek the rulebook, the treasure trove, the key to how to be that is passed down from father to son, from grandfather to grandchild.

In the same way that all the good boys really want to be bad, so all the bad boys dream of being good.

It is a physical thing. Like baby dragons in fantasy novels, young men are driven by the need to imprint as they cross the threshold into maturity and the cement begins to harden. Young men will seek champions in pop stars and film stars and sport stars chasing balls of various shapes and sizes. We need to attach ourselves to the great story. It is not about 'learning the possibilities of life' and 'knowing you can achieve your dream' but rather about How to Be. Through the millennia boys have received this instruction by observation, watching the older brother, watching the father, the uncle and the old men and, in the end, bonding with the other young men of the village to advance, to survive and to live the Story of Life.

I told Steve that I was just as lost as he was, that the 'coolness' was just in his mind and that I was human like him. I told him that I admired him because he had left school and apprenticed as a motor mechanic down at Robb's Motors in the city and was working Monday to Friday on Jaguars and Rolls-Royces and was going to be qualified early and would undoubtedly own his own business one day. If he had children they wouldn't go hungry.

He looked at me in surprise, or shock, and I could see the glimmer of a laugh at the corner of his eyes.

'You mean you are as fucked up as me?'

'No, I think I am perhaps more fucked up than you,' I admitted. 'That's why I like to hang around with you and Graeme and Dave, because you have something I don't have, and even if I will never have it, I like to be around it. So, really, I would like to learn to be more like you.'

I confided in him that I was afraid I would never get a real job and in the end I would become a *bergie*, sleeping on the mountain and walking barefoot, my tattered pants held up with string, looking for cigarette *entjies* in the gutters of my own home town. It was my greatest fear. He said that would never happen. He looked me in the eye and guaranteed me: 'I will always have a place for you to sleep in my house.' So over the years, silly as it may sound, it always kept me a little warmer under the cold foreign skies, knowing that if I ever made it home, there would still be some place for me to sleep.

I kept moving, out of the city and up towards the mountain, to the house where I'd stayed with Bridget and the girls. There were other people there now but they let me stay in my old room. It was too freaky, and I couldn't sleep. Someone had absconded with my bed and I curled up in the corner of the empty room. I would lie there all night long listening for cars, for car doors, for footsteps, expecting at any moment the door to be kicked in. Was it random that the cops raided that party and took all my friends? Did they already know that I was back in town?

Finally I met with Mr Pickwick, a Cool Cat from the Lucky City, a brother of the Other Brothers, a thespian par excellence and the man who taught the Devil how to talk sexy. He arranged for me to stay at his father's cottage down on Clifton Beach, the beach of all beaches, where I had spent so many of my teenage years, swimming, riding the waves on my lilo and, as I got older, partying at night up at the Clifton Hotel where the bands rocked on. It was the middle of winter and all the bikini babes were long gone, but it was a good winter beach, the grey overhead, the huge pounding dumper waves. It was like the mountain and the fog. Beautiful poetry weather. The cottage was called Golden Sunset and it lived up to its name.

Now that was home. I had never lived on that side of the city but it felt like home to me. Mr Pickwick's father lived upstairs and had his own trip and left me to my own devices. I was given a key to my private entrance and shown the lay of the land, including a fridge stocked top to bottom with nothing but beer. A fridge of beer on Clifton Beach instead of lying in some stinky prison drinking toilet water and waiting, waiting, measuring out my moments in cigarettes. If you put all the cigarettes you ever smoked, on the ground, end to end...?

'Just help yourself, Dad,' drawled the Prince of Cool to me, and then he suggested that I give him my useless expired passport. 'My old man knows some cat, some *goodie* in immigration who can maybe *make like that*, you knoooow, and get you a new deck, a full hand, maybe even a Royal Flush. Needless to say, you'll be back in the game.'

I gave him my passport and relaxed into the lifestyle, getting up early in the morning, knocking back a beer and going out into the cold surf to meet the sun as it came over the mountain and hit the sea. The beach was totally empty except for the memories of my youth, more ghosts dancing in the wind as the heavy seas drove the sand over the rocks where thousands of coins, fugitives from the pockets and purses of the last summer, were filtered, given back, glistening in the morning sun.

After a week or so of relaxing we went to the little clothing factory in Woodstock that Mr Pickwick senior owned and I shook his hand and he gave me my passport, somehow legally renewed with the help of a case of Chivas Regal, the official palm greaser of apartheid. I was counting down and facing the exit, the product of a team of human beings, strangers to each other, who had all passed the test.

I was back in The Game.

★★★★★★★★★★★ **30** ★★★★★★★★★★★

WHEN YOU GO AWAY

A blank page. White paper. Empty. Waiting for words. Emptiness waiting to be born. A child of imagination. This is an old song.

There were things, currents, undercurrents in the world of my family as a little boy, and on the outside pinging on my life like a distant sonar signal were all those world events, those pop songs and cold wars, the Suez Canal, the Cuban crisis, those tut-tutting little old ladies looking down their noses at our shameless Display of No Money. You lived, heard, saw, felt all those undercurrents of the big world swirling out there like the clouds in the sky, like the wind blowing down the face of the mountain, a storm waiting to break.

When you are a child, no matter how you live, traipsing from one side of the country to the other in ancient convertibles, walking when all the others are driving, wearing old clothes, living in dilapidated rented houses, paying money to fat old ladies who own half the block while living off their dead husband's investments, everything can still be okay because you're part of a family. You feel above them all when you have the magic. It is an ancient magic that has made itself apparent through hundreds of thousands, millions of years. A mother and a father and some kids – a family. It is a strong magic, that tribal blood bond, the building block of nations and societies. Egypt. China. Ireland. Afghanistan. Manitoba. Nature in motion. That is the total universe of the child. It is complete, eternal and unchanging. It is safety. In that world you can run and hide, you can dream and wish; you can follow the whims of your thought patterns and read books, play games, wander around in parks and lanes aimlessly kicking rocks, or just pick stalks of long grass to chew while lying on your back in the sun.

The undercurrents. The inner currents. There was often conflict of some sort in our family, but it always went away.

Then you look, you turn your head and you see. The undercurrent is a big rising swell and you hold your breath and try to float above it. You can swim. Even in a storm you can swim. Hold your head high. Even when the rain beats down and darkness falls and you have no life jacket and the ship has sunk out of view and all the little twinkling lights are gone, you can swim, kicking your little feet, keeping your mouth closed as you ride the great swells in the cold dark night, alone in the ocean, waiting for help to come. You can swim for your life.

Sometimes help doesn't come. Sometimes there is no Bridget to Dance with the Devil and no Samson to push aside the columns in the Temple of Doubt.

Swimming was the first freedom I discovered in this life. I never became a great swimmer or entered contests or anything. I just liked the magic. I must have been about five years old, and we would have walked from Fish Hoek along the old Main Road past Clovelly and on to St James, one of the most beautiful seaside walks in the world, especially if you are a child, but of course if you are a child then any walk is a magnificent adventure.

We walked past Clovelly where my father sat for a whole year painting the sun over the ocean in the morning and the complimentary shaft of light riding the ocean at sunset. Great big globs of oil paint in every kind of weather. You could actually see the weather in the paint, the sand gritty and grainy, blasted into the picture as he worked, or the subtle downward lines created by falling rain, or the cracked heat of the summer days.

At St James, so British in its architecture, so dreamily colonial, there is a pool constructed in the rocks right on the ocean, so when the tide comes in the waves crash over the pool. We always walked, my mother pushing the Little Guy in a pram, and we'd paddle in the water and play in the rock pools, as kids do, with seashells, fish, octopus, jellyfish, bluebottles, mussels, seaweed and dreams.

Sometimes we would run around the edge of the pool, where people were always swimming. I stood on the edge of that whitish square around the inviting cool water, the sun like a searchlight exploding in my face, reflecting and refracting in a billion small ripples. I could see into the sweet green liquid, the churning froth of bubbles where a man had just dived into the water and out of this world, this world where we stood, where the sun beat down, where the earth was so dry that cattle were dying all over the country, so hot that you just had to look at the mountain and another fire would start.

But under there in the water the man arced his body and floated without wings in another dimension, his arms outstretched, back curved, like a prayer, a magical holy moment, as he glided on and on and then broke through the surface in a sudden thrashing of fresh and energetic bubbles.

I had seen people doing this before, but never really looked very closely. This time I saw it all, how they stood with their toes almost curling over the edge, poised with knees slightly bent, a springing motion of faith as the body launched gracefully into the air as if to fly and then, suddenly changing its destination, down through the wall of water into the secret underworld of wingless flying. I watched and I learned.

My mother was keeping a keen eye on me in case I fell in. My brother was looking too. I stood on the edge of the pool and I flew into the air and then down through the window and out of the world of heavy heat, hard surfaces and gravity, and as I went down I flew up, I broke free of the only dimension I had ever known. That was my first religious experience, when I gave myself willingly with faith to that pool of water, that tiny fraction of the oceans that cover this planet, in communion with life, twisting like a dolphin. Feeling beatific. I became an acolyte of water. It felt like I was going home in some way, like an ancient memory. I knew the water and it knew me. From that day I spent a large portion of my life always in or near the water. I could swim. I could fly. Water was a waking, sensuous dream of luxury.

My poor mother jumped up, ready to save me, but when she realised that I was actually swimming she bristled with pride.

Of course that was just a pool. There were no rip tides, tsunamis or killer sharks. It was a safe place, just like home. In my home there was not much money, it is true, but there was also no second-hand cigarette smoke or drunkenness. There was no violence, except for the repeated pummelling from my older sibling. Even though the family teetered on the edge of total scandalous poverty it was still a place a child could dream in the safe knowledge that the bigger people were there, like the safe walls of the pool where I taught myself to swim on that day of discovery. I didn't notice the quiet desperation of our existence, the lack of a greater family circle, the extended family, the village, just like I didn't notice the Cold War or the Mandela trials. I was in my own dream in my own swimming pool.

But tsunamis do come to peaceful beaches, earthquakes do happen on quiet summer evenings, wars come to villages when children are writing exams, plagues decimate continents and fires eradicate cities on little girls' birthdays, and no matter how solidly your house was built, the world around you does fall into uncontrollable, irrevocable chaos. Sometimes.

I was lying in my bed in that old room upstairs on Moray Place. It was a small room with a door that had ancient panels of multi-coloured stained glass from some bygone era around the Boer War, a door that led on to an old balcony. One of the small glass panels was broken and had a little square of hardboard nailed over it. When the wind blew down the mountain, that door would shake as if the devil and all his zombies were out there and the whole house would shudder. Trees would fall, and I remember sometimes a square van or a VW Kombi would blow right over. If you walked up the mountain when that wind blew, it would take the breath right out of your mouth if you didn't wear a mask.

My father came to see me as I lay there in my bed. I couldn't see the mountain any more, because they had just built a block of flats across the road from us on the empty ground where we used to play soldiers. Sometimes my father would come to say goodnight to me. I liked that. This time, as I lay there in the dark, twelve years old, on the verge of change, he said he had to tell me something.

'I am going to move out,' he said, 'to live somewhere else for a little while, but it won't be for that long. Just a short while.'

'Okay,' I said, as he kissed my childhood goodbye and went away.

But it was okay, because I knew that he was coming back. It would just be a short while, and even though everything was upside down, and my mother was angry with me a lot, saying that my disruptive behaviour was the cause of his departure, even though I had to stand up at school when they asked everybody who was too poor to buy their own books to stand up and be humiliated publicly, I knew it would all be okay, and I treaded water, faithfully waiting for him to come back and rescue us.

It was a long time before I realised that he hadn't told me the truth and that he wasn't coming back.

He might have forgotten saying those words as soon as he walked out the door. It was easier to lie, easier for him, not understanding that he was giving me false hope, something that I could cling to in times of trouble. Maybe he was lying to himself too. He was raised by a single mother, his big Boer father living up on the family orange farm in the Eastern Cape with his new wife, so maybe my father didn't know what a father was supposed to do, besides go away, and perhaps he just did what he was trained to do, what his father had done, and went away, leaving his new people twisting in the wind, in pursuit of self-fulfilment.

Jacques Brel, Shirley Bassey, Dusty Springfield. Ne me quitte pas. When you go away ... when you go away. Those are words with a melody. Something sluggish on the bottom end, slow and turgid but never anchored.

When someone dies they go away and never come back. That's the way it works. When someone very close to you dies you wake up every morning and, once again, the person who was there every day is still gone. Gone away. Forever. The solid unchangeable truth. Grief.

When you are young and desperate it seems so easy just to give the finger and say, 'Fuck you and all your lot.' When you don't know yourself you think you can do anything. In my head I thought I could just weather it all, hold my breath and come out okay on the other side, jump in the lake of time, close my eyes, hold my breath, and swim hard towards the future.

I had walked country roads and mountain paths, I had hitch-hiked so many times up and down the coast and through the interior. I had slept in fields and ditches, at petrol stations and in the back of bakkies. I had slept upon the earth and rolled in its fullness. I had marvelled at high hills and open orange landscapes with strange purple mountains. Gravel, heat and the sounds of many languages, the smells of different peoples. I was only twenty-one and had seen more of the land than many had, but there was so much more, so much I still hadn't touched. My body and the earth had mingled so closely, but my mind, my brain, thought I could just go away. When you go away.

Before this prison shit, I *wanted* to get away, away from the army and the apartheid dream, to some place civilised. Now I *had* to get away. There was no more choice. I was branded: criminal on the run. My options were severely whittled down. I was fucked, well and truly fucked, and unless I wanted to become a professional lawbreaker, a bandit hiding in the mountains, I had to go. In the Sunday papers every so often were stories of criminals speaking through a reporter, wanting to surrender, looking for peace, with lurid headlines and tragic details.

I still had this bizarre hope that I could get a real life, go to a university and get a job and pay rent and buy stuff with my money and go on holidays. In order to accomplish this I had to go away into the void of the other world. What world? I had no foreign relatives that I knew of, just an internationally reviled South African passport, now beautifully renewed and useful thanks to a man who shook my hand and asked no more, and a birth certificate that declared me to be *manlik* and *blank*. What prospects did I have as an illegal alien in other lands? I had no counsel. Nobody to offer me advice or sanctuary. No school. No visa. No plan. Just a small bag of hope and a pocketful of wishes.

In the middle of winter I walked up the gangplank of the Union-Castle ship, the *Edinburgh Castle*, and presented the immigration officer with my ticket and my passport, a document with my real name in it. It sounds so simple now, but I was a Wanted Escaped Lunatic Criminal (to be precise) on the run, and right there, at the passport-control guy, was one of the traps where they snared little stinky mice like me. If there was a list of hunted felons, all he had to do was scan it alphabetically and if I was on it nod at some hidden cop who would drag me away.

Come on, mousey, take the cheese. Look, it's perfectly harmless. Come on, little mouse, we are waiting... But I had to take a chance. I suppose I could have tried Swaziland or gone north through Africa, but there was war along all the borders. South West Africa, Angola, Rhodesia, Mozambique. All were filled with war. Guns. Fire. Troops. Police. Mines.

I was such a hungry mouse.

Mousey, mousey.

A gentle breeze was blowing, and all around were throngs of people, little family groups. The atmosphere was festive, with porters and taxi drivers and uniformed personnel bustling to and fro. There was laughing and talking and groups on the dock were already waving at others leaning over the railing. Cameras flashed. Women cried and laughed. Coloured streamers curled through the air.

This was the only way. I knew of no other way out. Once again a moment when you roll the dice. You wait. You think. You plan and sweat and think and wish it were all different and that this was just a dream. You cry at night for the wasted life you see ahead of you and then you step out like a gunslinger in *High Noon*, like a Zulu warrior into the cannon of the British. A little dramatic? Why don't you try it, and then come and talk to me again about 'drama', about impeccably crippling tension.

As a kid, I always wondered if I could do those things. I was always worrying about getting hurt. But a time comes when you must make your move. You lie quaking from the fear. Every night-time noise, every car door, could be them coming to take you, to beat you, to lock you up in their places of filth. Anybody could be a betrayer. So many were.

On the docks, the old grey concrete was criss-crossed with railway lines, filled with splinters and chips from countless wooden pallets, and lined with massive cranes busily loading cargo from the warehouses. I knew the smell of those warehouses. I knew the whole area. It was the smell of the dying days of my innocence. I used to run there with my little friends from District Six when I was a boy and we were the kings of all we surveyed, fishing and laughing, totally unaware of the sad truth that the future held for us.

The night before leaving my broken life, I'd lain in bed, unable to sleep, my head filled with visions of myself running down that desolate dock, gunfire popping as the bullets stained my back with heat and my life left me lying alone on the cool grey concrete, inhaling the odour of oil and wood chips. I loved that smell. I was so tired and I just wanted to lie down on that cold concrete that had seen so many comings and goings. I just wanted to lie down and cry.

One chance. Just walk up the plank. Roll the dice.

There was no internet and no fax back then. Just telephones. Perhaps it's because I was the responsibility of Sterkfontein mental hospital when I escaped, and maybe there was a lack of interdepartmental communication. Perhaps there were rivalries between certain arms and wings and sects of the government and the civil service.

Perhaps because I was a madman they didn't think I would have the skills to get all the way south and then onto a boat. Perhaps, perhaps, perhaps.

Roll the dice. Step off the cliff and hope that the sweet mother of your fate will catch you before you fall to your doom, crushed on the pitiless rocks of your pathetic life. Of course my actual flesh-and-blood mother is right there with me, distracting the passport officer with a big bunch of flowers in his face, asking if it's okay if they come on board, she and the young lady, and if there is some kind of warning that will let her know when the ship is about to leave.

'Yes, madam, there will be an announcement.' He just wants her to move the flowers so he can check out the tight T-shirt on the *lekker stukkie* with the bleached blonde hair and the short denim skirt who is holding my bag. I'd met her a few days earlier on Clifton Beach, the last of the beautiful girls from this city. I swear the immigration guy doesn't even look at my passport.

'Thank you, sir. Have a nice voyage.'

A nice voyage? A new life? (I made it! I made it! I made it!)

Fucking cunts!

Fucking cunts. I made it. All those dark nights lying sleepless with the End of My Life throbbing in my skull, planning, wishing and hoping, plotting revenge with dentist drills in the ears of all the betrayers and backstabbers, but never really believing, or maybe never really giving up. It was impossible, but there I was, on the deck of a ship with a one-way ticket to some place called Las Palmas, wherever that was. Have a nice fucking voyage indeed. Enjoy your first steps into the void away from everything you ever knew. Enjoy the lonely silence of your own heart breaking.

The Greatest Trek of all.

This was the next level in the game, away from my world and never again to see Squeaky, Donny, Deadly Hedley, the Charlie-Bird, Bridget, Samson, Poison Pete, Long Street Steve, my family, my trees, the birds and all the things I did not yet even comprehend ... away to where Zulu people are mythical creatures in books, away from bunny chows and samoosas made the proper way. My father. Never again to walk the streets of my home town barefoot under the shadow of the mountain. My instruments. All the beautiful girls. The smell of the mountain when winter comes. My silly old dog that I had left at my mother's house years before. Every. Thing.

It hadn't hit me yet. The sky was grey and I settled into the deepest, cheapest cabin without a window. I had a girl on my arm and yellow Cape see-through wine in a bottle. My mother had brought me proteas, a big bunch, a big symbol of all I thought I wished to forget and never see again. What was she feeling? Perhaps relief because, after all, she had arranged the money and the ticket for me. Without her I would have had to sink deeper to make more money to get out. The terrible spiral into a world of doom. She had raised money here and there from every person she could think of. She had even phoned my Boer grandfather, the mysterious Oupa Piet up there in Johannesburg, where he had been working as the headmaster of a high school since they let him out of the nuthouse. He must have had some good connections to get a little appointment like that.

My grandfather's second wife told my mother that the old man was sick, too sick to help me in any way, and the shock, the knowledge of this disgrace, could possibly kill him. Would it kill him to do even one little thing for me – his grandson? It would seem so.

But what did my mother see? What did she think of me? Did she think I was really crazy or an amoral criminal who would stoop to any low activity? Did she think she would never see me again? Her son. Her troubled darling one for whom she'd had so much hope: only twenty-one years old and pretty much fucked for good. But who knows? Who knows what could happen out there in 'the rest of the world'? It was difficult for me too, mostly because I knew she didn't see my version of the movie. In her head she saw her version, where the country wasn't 'as bad as all that'. I should have been wondering when, or if, I would see her again. I hadn't had time to really think about going away on all levels, who I would owe and who I would miss. I just had to go, now, and sometime in the future I would sit down and think. Put the fucking emotions on hold. It was more like I was on a countdown, the moments electric and dull at the same time.

We knew that the boat would leave at such and such a time. We made light chatter and sipped the wine. Then they left, my mother and the girl, and my head hurt. Just like in prison, the visitors had to leave for my sentence to begin. When I thought of my family I felt so conflicted and the grey cloud came into my head. I looked at them and saw no way out, no way I could help them or do anything for them. Depression is a tricky little bastard sometimes. And I felt so bad for always letting them down from the very beginning, always doing the wrong thing.

I stood on the top deck wearing the sheepskin coat Deadly Hedley had given me, the big brown woollen scarf from my mother around my neck, as the boat sailed out of the Duncan Dock. I saw her at the end of the breakwater by the small lighthouse where I had often fished alone as a boy, never catching anything but mud sharks. A small figure waving. It is a moment we always remember, my mother Shirley and me.

THE BEGINNING

Walking with a Mountain. Mott the Hoople.
On the weekends in Cape Town, people would get in their cars and drive here and there, out into the country and to the hot spots, the holiday venues, all the beautiful places up and down the coast or inland. Cars insulate you in your protected metal worlds. They get you places and they buy you freedom.

The rubber tyres insulate you electrically from the earth. When we get into our vehicles, our chariots, we rise up and look down on the small creatures, liberated finally from the pedestrian life, too good for the earth – aristocrats, progressives, better, better, better. To be a pedestrian in the modern world is to be a study in not having, as you watch other people zipping by in their happiness, getting from where they were to where they want to be all in a flash. You stand. You look, waiting at the bus stop, standing in the rain, holding your mother's hand. The haves and the have-nots. The living and the ghostly. So easy to be seduced, lured into desiring the grand expanses of happiness acquired by the beautiful vehicle.

But something is lost when our turn comes and we step up, higher than the very earth, zooming here and there, drinking from our taps and ordering our things from servants and wage slaves. The world becomes a television show, you the consumer, choosing the pieces you wish to enjoy, taking little bits from here and there for your pleasure.

With our cars and our jets we can go so fast that we break the sound barrier and maybe one day it will be the light barrier and we will all zoom away into the cosmos looking for new places to conquer and exploit or just another place to hide from ourselves. But to break the memory barrier you have to slow down.

You have to stop running and wait for the past to catch up with you.

Remember the rhythm of walking the long walk. Not going for a toddle, a stroll, stepping out to take some air, get some exercise, but the long walk. It is a different speed, a completely different life to the driver who is living in a world of connected events all linked together by motor journeys. He has almost eradicated the middle part, the annoying part, the getting there.

Walking is like hand-to-hand combat. It requires effort and hard use of the human body. After thousands of years of fighting among men, some bright guys came up with the arrow, the bow, the crossbow and then the gun and all its penile extensions and homoerotic metaphors. You could now kill without ever meeting, without any chance of being hurt yourself. It was more efficient, and battles became measured by the body count. The story changed, because the middle part was taken out. There was nothing left but death and propaganda.

Was it not the middle part that gave the event of war some meaning in the days of the heroes, the warrior with his weapon sweaty in his hand, running, screaming, crying, cutting, killing, falling, living and dying, in combat, in mortal marriage, hand to hand? You had to work for your kill, and it was the honest toil that gave that terrible event some grace, some poetry, some honour. Stories were written. Songs were sung.

And so it is with walking. We did it for so long: for thousands upon thousands of years we walked across the great plains, up into the mountains and down through the dry riverbeds. We walked to battle and we walked home, weary but victorious, with our dead upon our shoulders. We walked and we ran. We chased enemies and animals and they, in turn, chased us. The earth was always here and we walked together always connected.

When you walk you touch the earth, and when you walk barefoot you caress it. The earth is a great big battery and we are a hundred billion light bulbs waiting to be plugged in. When you walk day in and day out, you move at a different pace, an ancient pace that is synchronised rhythmically with your inner self. There was a time, a few hundred years before, when the European settlers found the Village under the great Table Mountain a desirable and fashionable place to live, so, after clearing out the freed slaves and *hotnots* who lived there, on the sides of the mountain, they built fancy houses and parks and bandstands. But that was long before, and in my youth the heart of the brick city that they'd named Kaapstad, Cape Town, had been mostly deserted by the fashionable elite, who had moved out to more desirable suburbs.

When you live in the heart of the Old City the mountain is always the dominating presence, like a parent. Over everything is the mountain. On weekends my parents would take us walking up Orange Street, past the upper water reservoir and past St Cyprians Girl's School and up a path next to a silver stream, out of the neighbourhoods and up through the trees past the mountain ranger's house and past the graves of the holy Muslim prophets with their whitewashed stones and fresh silks, and up further, over rocks and past the stands of cactus with their purple spiked prickly pears that my father showed us how to eat by rolling them in the gravel, and, always following the water, the river that I dreamed ran under our house at number ten Moray Place, we walked and walked till we were well into the belly of the mountain, where there was the ghost of a broken foundation of an ancient building long gone, and we would set up camp and start a fire.

We played in the trees and in the river. We ran around collecting porcupine quills, eating wild gooseberries and nuts from pine cones and sucking on sourflowers. We cooked our food on hot coals and filled our jugs with mountain water to take home to drink. For three or four years we did those things – my father, mother and the four children, still a family. If my father was away working or climbing a mountain, my mother would take us on her own. We became mountain children.

Sometimes we would walk for miles along the Pipe Track, traversing the lower slope till we got to Kloof Nek, between the mountain and Lion's Head, and we would go down through The Glen and down to Camps Bay Beach. In those years our feet became intimately involved with the Every Where. We walked and walked and walked and the land loved our little bare feet. It talked to our feet.

We seemed to be the only family who were on the mountain all the time. We never saw anybody else making fires and eating food. It was just 'not done'. Sometimes we'd see some people walking the Pipe Track or going mountain climbing, on an excursion, but they would get in their cars, their Vauxhalls, Rovers and Opels, their Ford Fairlanes, Jaguars and Fiats, and drive to a parking lot from where they would start the hike, return and then drive to their next diversion.

The world had changed, and the in-between bits, the way we got from place to place, which had always been a story in itself, often an epic, they were gone. The way we travelled in time had changed. Efficiency was gained and poetry was lost in the irreversible power exchange.

In the time before, before experience and memory led to the naming of things, giving pre-loaded meaning to existence, turning footsteps into words, transforming the is-ness of eternity into a manageable sense of place; before all the mountains of the world, there was only this one mountain. Before Mounts Vesuvius, Ararat or Kilimanjaro. Before Everest or Aconcagua. Before Mount Rushmore, Mount Olympus or Mount Zion. Before all the holy mountains of the world were named, there was this place, the name known now perhaps only in the Secret Village, I can't say, I have been gone far too long and I forget the way – not that I'm lost, I know exactly where I am, I just can't find my way there – but, if you translated that name into English, it would most probably be something simple like ... home.

Old, old spirits held sway on the slopes of that mountain, whispering among their lonely selves while dreaming of their children, all the human beings who once were theirs. Their peoples were all gone and their trees had all been chopped down, to build furniture, tables and chairs, the last of the ancient woods, carried in wagons like slaves to distant places in the north, and in their place had been brought northern trees, pines and oaks, which took root and grew like tall greedy weeds across the face of the old mountain. And those trees were sad too, in the bright heat of the southern sun so far from their dreams of snow and ice-blue nights.

While other families went to Hermanus, Knysna, London, Namaqualand, New York or Hout Bay, we walked deeper and deeper into the Secret Village. We became part of the landscape and the land welcomed us home. The old spirits, I have to admit, doted on us, in the way that old people whose children are gone dote on dogs and budgies. There was a time when they were the centre, surrounded by so many happy children in their ancient garden, too many to count in one day, and they were the heart of the unchanging dream, but all they had in my time was us, and they adopted us, as lost as we were, cultural bastards spat out from the colonial meat grinder that absent-mindedly chewed up Life in the name of progress, power and profit.

I would take off my shoes, my sandals, takkies or floppies, and walk barefoot even on the hot tar of the Old City. On super-hot days the tar would get soft in places and you could leave a footprint in the melted pavement. There is a warmth that spreads to the very bones, the core of my existence, just remembering.

My two favourite sensations always were the yin and yang of temperature, my fondness for soaking up heat through my soles from the earth and then the release of diving into the ocean in a rush of icy cold. Suspended. Graceful. Charge and release. Simple pleasures.

There are so many bad dreams I wished, still wish, I could have taken back from my mother's experience and memory. So many sleepless nights and terrible times, and not enough of the other ones. The moments a mother swells with pride when her child learns to hold a spoon and feed itself, and, moving through the years, to win a foot race or a school prize. It is more than pride; it is a sigh of relief when you realise that the child is slowly gaining the ability to exist, survive and succeed in life with both peers and the world in general.

From the deck of the ship I could see my whole life, spread out in a panorama: Devil's Peak, Table Mountain, the city, the Bo-Kaap, Lion's Head and Signal Hill, all covered top to bottom and left to right with hundreds of little stories that added up to my life, my history, my sense of place.

But … I was still alive, not in prison and not in the army killing fellow humans, not pushing people around, not making old people and children cry, and I had not intentionally betrayed anybody, except possibly myself.

I know that I was just one guy on my own in my battle, my private war for my country, whatever that was, and for my people, whoever they were. I was running away, but I felt that I had put my body on the line in the only way that I knew, and, somewhere in the middle of the bad choices, the stumbling logic, the search for a thread of truth, I had headed in the right direction, because the core issue to me was not family, mental illness, law-breaking, cowardice, bravery, drugs or crime. It was killing.

As a teenager, when I ingested the post-war propaganda that passed for entertainment, I saw that all the killers pointed upwards, saying: 'I could not stop. They told me to do it. My superiors would have hurt me, so instead I hurt others.' The Nuremberg defence. The Nazi defence.

'God told me to do it' and 'God told me to tell you to do it.' The Moses defence.

I thought it was wrong and that every man and woman should take responsibility for their own actions, or all you get is another Great War, with tens of millions dead who were too ashamed or afraid to just say no. It seemed like such impeccable Maths. How do you give up smoking? You don't pick up a cigarette. How do you give up war?

So that's it. That is the word problem that was given to me at the beginning of this exam. To kill or not to kill? It sounds so simple if you have a Mathematical Mind. The answer is obvious to all human beings, but, you know the teacher – s/he always wants to see all the work, and wants to know that you really understand the Mechanics of the Mathematical Problem, wants to see you apply known theorems – and, who knows, you might even do something the teacher hadn't thought of. So, that is what I have attempted to do here, show my work. It's a little messy, I know, but that's probably because I am left-handed and I am always a little nervous during tests.

Had I passed the test or had I failed? Was I good or was I bad? I will never know, because I wasn't there when they gave out the prizes. I was barely twenty-one years old and it was to be another twenty-one years before I saw my home town again. As the city slid from view I headed below deck in search of a bar. I just wanted to drink. I didn't realise that I was supposed to fall to my knees and weep, but there was plenty of time for that …

ACKNOWLEDGEMENTS

Often when telling one story, a grander one can sweep you away.

Firstly, I would like to say thank you to publisher Marlene Fryer, whose enthusiasm gave life to this project from the beginning, and to all the gang at Zebra Press in Cape Town for their excellent work.

There is a lot I could never get done without the support of my wife Mary Ann and her amazing ability to cater to and deal with my creative whims and strange hours year in and year out.

I am very grateful for the hot tips, the early reads and the nuggets of advice, help and encouragement around the edges from Paddy Gillard-Bentley, Revel Fox, Dave Herron, Alex Deeth, Mbanya Dube, Ingrid Thompson, Gillian Levy, Trish Brown, Uaanavi Tjitunga, Jesse Finkelstein, Arkansas Delacroix, Jonny Steinberg, Alex Alberro and Mike Nicol.

Unfortunately, very shortly after signing the book contract with Marlene I was hospitalised with cancer, acute leukaemia, and spent six weeks on a bed with tubes and machines, followed by three months more of chemotherapy. I am extremely grateful to the staff (except for that stupid shrink and the creepalicious French doctor of course) of the Leukaemia and Bone Marrow Transplant team on T15 and in the Krall Centre at Vancouver General Hospital for their wonderful care and expertise and for keeping me in this world so that I could get a few more things done.

Totally coincidentally, the day after my chemotherapy ended, editor Robert Plummer emailed from ten thousand miles away to tell me that we were going to work. Today! We were a month behind our original start time, and deadlines were looming. No time to lie back and think of ... bad things. I had lost all focus while getting toxic in hospitals for months and had really done no work at all. Robert came in like a forensic detective, going over every single word for clues and raising hundreds of uncomfortable questions. I supplied the answers and we slowly filled in the blanks. Thanks to his boundless patience, perceptiveness and uncanny feel for flow, we rearranged my scattered thoughts and loose chronology to create a coherent finished product.

ERICH RAUTENBACH
VANCOUVER, JUNE 2011

TRANSLATIONS

p. 4   *Finish an' klaa' my bra!*
       Finished and done, my brother!

p. 27 Little *donders*, the police will *moer* you. Out! *Voertsek!*
       Little troublemakers, the police will beat you up. Out! Fuck off!

p. 33 *Wie's jy? Ken jy vir die ding? Wut you wunt waaitie?*
       Who're you? Do you know this thing? What you want, whitey?

p. 34 *twee rand vyftig vir die arm*
       two rand fifty for the parcel

       Hie's 'n paar koppe vir jou, Blondie.
       Here are a few heads for you, Blondie.

p. 37 Hey, Luminous, *hoe ga'dit? Waar's jou fokken hoedjie?*
       Eh, Luminous, how's it going? Where's your fucking hat?

p. 50 *Is hy dood?*
       Is he dead?

p. 51 *ek lewe nog, meneer.*
       I'm still alive, mister.

THE UNEXPLODED BOER

p. 69   Hey, Luminous, *waar's jou fokken hoedjie?*
Eh, Luminous, where's your fucking hat?

Jy, waaaai-tie, give me a *dop* there *ek sê.*
Hey, whitey, give me a drink there, I say.

p. 89   *Jy sal later betaal.*
You'll pay later.

p. 121   *E'sê vir hom ... sy ma se fok se moer ... jou tief-naai jentoe!*
I said to him ... his mother's fucking cunt ... you bitch-fuck prostitute!

p. 143   *Ag,* come on my *boet,* shoot me a *entjie asseblief ... Ek het niks hier.*
Oh, come on my brother, shoot me a cigarette please ... I've got nothing here.

Nay man ... ek ook ou maat. Ons is nou saam diep in'ie kak.
No man ... me too old friend. Now we're deep in the shit together.

p. 144   *Jou ma se moer ...* All I got to do is *moer* you *sat* and I go home one-time *ek sê.*
Your mother's cunt ... All I got to do is beat you senseless and I go home one-time I say.

Fok you, *jou ma se moer, jou befokte boer!*
Fuck you, your mother's cunt, you fucking Afrikaner!

p. 158   *Ja, maar hy is pragtig vandag, u Edelagbare.*
Yes, but he is pretty today, Your Worship.

p. 163   *Jirre Jissus in sy befokte moer!*
Lord Jesus in his fucking cunt!

p. 202   *Jou ma se fok se moer, Vorster!*
Your mother's fucking cunt, Vorster!

GLOSSARY

acid: LSD
ag: oh
baas: boss
babelas: hung-over
baie kak: very shit
bakkie: pickup truck
befokte mapuza: fucking police
bergie: homeless person
bittereinders: Boer guerrillas who vowed to fight to the bitter end
blank: white
blow tjonna: blow smoke through a mouthful of wine
Boer: Afrikaner
boer: farmer, police
Boerbefok: crazy-fuck Boer
boerewors: sausage
boertjie: little policeman
boet: brother
Bo-Kaap: traditionally Muslim neighbourhood above Cape Town
bonny: hair
bonsela: bonus
borrel see-through: bottle of unlabelled wine
BOSS: Bureau of State Security
boy: black or brown man (derogatory)

bra/blaaah: brother
braai: barbecue
brak: mongrel
breker: tough suburban Afrikaner
broer, broeder: brother
Bronx, the: Hillbrow
bru: brother
bundu: the bush
bunny chow: hollowed-out loaf of bread filled with curry
Casspir: armoured combat vehicle
china: mate, friend
Compagnie: Company (Dutch East India Company)
dagga: marijuana
dexies: dextroamphetamines (uppers)
die kind van die wind: the child of the wind
District, the: District Six
doek: scarf
dominee: minister
donders: troublemakers
dop: drink
dos: sleep
droëwors: dried sausage
droit de seigneur: the lord's right
Durban Poison: potent marijuana from KwaZulu-Natal
Egoli: Place of Gold, referring to Johannesburg
ek sê: I say
entjie: cigarette butt
finish an' klaa: finished and done
Flats, the: Cape Flats
fok: fuck
fokken: fucking
ganja: marijuana
gartjie: little guard
gat: hole, arse

geelrys: yellow rice, a Cape Malay dish
geld: money
gif: poison; marijuana
gofer: dogsbody
goffels: schoolboy slang for black guys
gogga: insect, bug
Green Goblin: type of LSD
gunston: a brand of cigarette; slang for marijuana
hensopper: hands-upper; Boer fighters who surrendered during the Anglo-Boer War
harders: kind of fish
hardloop: run
hierdie kakland: this shitland
hoedjie: little hat
hotnot: shortened form of 'Hottentot'
howzit: how's it
Ikey: University of Cape Town
ja: yes
jislaaik: wow
jol: party
joller: party animal
Jozi: Johannesburg
kaffer (Afrikaans), **kaffir** (English): derogatory term for black person
kafferboetie: kaffir-lover
kak: shit
katkop: literally cat's head; hunk of wholewheat bread
Kerk Plein: Church Square
Khoikhoi: original inhabitants of South Africa
Kombi: Volkswagen people-carrier
Kullid: my own version of the insulting word 'coloured'
Kunjani? Uthini?: How are you? Pardon?
kwela-kwela: police van
laaitie: youngster
lang-gat jollers: big-time party animals

lanieskap: genteel society
lekker gerook: nice and stoned
lekker stukkie: tasty piece (of the female variety)
lilo: floating air mattress
manlik and blank: male and white
manne: the boys
mano a mano: hand to hand
mapuza: police
marram: madam
mielies: corn
moer: murder, beat up (v.), cunt (n.)
muti: medicine
Mx: Mandrax
my blaaah: my brother (stretched-out street pronunciation of 'my bra')
nagmaal: evening meal, communion
Ne me quitte pas: Don't leave me
'n glim van 'n lag: a glimmer of a smile
'n ou aap van die Kaap: an old ape from the Cape
oke: guy
oom: uncle
ou: old, guy
ouma: grandmother
oupa: grandfather
pil: joint
poes: cunt
poesboekies: trashy photo stories about secret agents, romance and adventure
poeskas: cunt cupboard
poeslap: sanitary towel
Poison: Durban Poison, a kind of marijuana
polies kar: police car
potjie: cooking pot
pozi: place
rock up: show up

roker: smoker (of marijuana)
rooineks: derogatory term for English people, whose white skin burnt red in the sun; literally 'red necks'
samoosas: fried pastry snacks with spicy filling
SAP: South African Police
sat: thoroughly
see-through wine: unlabelled wine
sensimilla: seedless marijuana
shebeen: illegal township pub
sit vas: sit tight
skaapie: little sheep
skandaal: scandal
skelm: scoundrel
skollie: gangster
skyf: smoke
smokkelaar: smuggler
sout: salt
staunch connection: someone you can trust to look out for you
steenbras: type of fish
stoep: verandah
stompie: little stump
stoppe: finger-sized portions of marijuana
suiping: drinking
SWAPO: South West Africa People's Organisation
Taal: language (Afrikaans)
takkies: tennis shoes, sneakers
takhaar: hippie; wild hair, as if caught in tree branches
tannie: auntie
terrs: terrorists
three-blader: joint made with three cigarette papers
toe: closed
tsotsi: gangster
twak: tobacco
veld: the bush

verkrampte: conservative, intolerant
verlep ou poesface: saggy old cunt face
voertsek: get away, fuck off
vrou: woman, wife
vygie: type of succulent plant
Window Pane: type of LSD
zef: white lower-class style
zol: marijuana

SOURCES

'Five Years' (David Bowie)
Original Publishers: Screen Gems/EMI Music,
Chrysalis Music and Tintoretto Music.
Administered by EMI Music Publishing SA (Pty) Ltd and
Fairwood Music (Africa) (Pty) Ltd

'Simple Man' (Graham Nash)
Original Publisher: Nash Notes.
Administered by Sony/ATV Music Publishing

'I Shall Be Released' (Bob Dylan)
Original Publisher: Dwarf Music.
Administered by Sony/ATV Music Publishing

'Jean' (Rod McKuen)
Original Publisher: Warner Chappell Music Inc.
Administered by Gallo Music Publishers

'Midnight Rider' (Gregg Allman, Robert Payne)
Original Publishers: Elijah Blue Music and Warner Chappell Music Inc.
Administered by Geoff Paynter Music Publishing and Gallo Music Publishers

'Heroes' (David Bowie, Brian Eno)
Original Publishers: Screen Gems/EMI Music,
EG Music Publishing Ltd and Tintoretto Music.
Administered by EMI Music Publishing SA (Pty) Ltd, Universal Music Publishing
MGB Africa and Fairwood Music (Africa) (Pty) Ltd

'Death of a Clown' (Ray Davies, Dave Davies)
Original Publisher: (Artemis) Warner Chappell Music Ltd.
Administered by Gallo Music Publishers

Do you have any comments, suggestions or feedback about this book or any other Zebra Press titles? Contact us at **talkback@zebrapress.co.za**